CASE STUDIES IN

CULTURAL ANTHROPOLOGY

GENERAL EDITORS

George and Louise Spindler

STANFORD UNIVERSITY

THE FORGOTTEN FRONTIER

Ranchers of North Brazil

THE FORGOTTEN FRONTIER

Ranchers of North Brazil

PETER RIVIÈRE

Cambridge University

HOLT, RINEHART AND WINSTON, INC.

NEW YORK   CHICAGO   SAN FRANCISCO   ATLANTA

DALLAS   MONTREAL   TORONTO   LONDON   SYDNEY

Foreword

About the Series

These case studies in cultural anthropology are designed to bring to students, in beginning and intermediate courses in the social sciences, insights into the richness and complexity of human life as it is lived in different ways and in different places. They are written by men and women who have lived in the societies they write about and who are professionally trained as observers and interpreters of human behavior. The authors are also teachers, and in writing their books they have kept the students who will read them foremost in their minds. It is our belief that when an understanding of ways of life very different from one's own is gained, abstractions and generalizations about social structure, cultural values, subsistence techniques, and the other universal categories of human social behavior become meaningful.

About the Author

Peter Rivière was born in London in 1934. He is married and has three children. He is currently a Lecturer at the Institute of Social Anthropology, University of Oxford, where he obtained his D.Phil. in 1965. He has previously held appointments in the Universities of Cambridge, Harvard and London. Dr. Rivière has done field work among the Carib-speaking Trio Indians of Surinam (1963–1964) and among the Brazilians who are the subject of this case study (1967). His publications include *Marriage among the Trio* (1969) and numerous articles on a variety of topics. He has recently edited a new edition of J. F. McLennan's *Primitive Marriage* (1970).

About the Book

Studies of frontier ranching communities in the New World are virtually nonexistent. Our own frontier and cowboy subcultures were never described ethnographically. Professor Rivière has given us a unique and detailed ethnography of the cattle ranching culture of Roraima in the most northerly part of Brazil. The study is an excellent example of the balance existing between man in socius and man in his ecosystem. The author describes how the Roraimaenses' socioeconomic organization and its concomitant values are enmeshed with a specific combination of historical, geographical, and environmental factors. This necessitates rather elaborate background materials on the natural environment and history of the area, which are included in the introductory chapters. With these data available, the reader is given an understanding of why the alternating wet and dry seasons, the terrain, the lack of railroads or traversable roads for many months of the year, the lack of available markets and centers of population, and the egalitarian socioeconomic system are intricately interrelated. And all of these aspects of culture and technology reflect the influence of cattle ranching.

Some interesting problems are posed for the student of peasant cultures. Students of Latin America regard livestock ranches as a subtype of the plantation subculture (Wagley & Harris) or a rural proletariat (Strickon), and neither description fits Roraima. Its population more closely approximates peasants as defined by Foster and Belshaw. Other students (Wolf) exclude livestock keepers in their definitions of peasant. The fit is, however, very loose, as the Roraimaenses have a limited interest in the market economy and their system could be described as subsistence ranching. But, the author queries, is it reasonable to describe as a peasant a man, who, if his assets were realizable, would be worth about half a million U.S. dollars? The problem of classification remains unsolved.

The Roraimaenses are further unique among Latin American communities in that social stratification in the usual sense is unknown here. There is neither a socioeconomic nor cultural break between the cowboy and a wealthy rancher. It is the ambition of every cowboy (vaqueiro) to become a rancher (fazendeiro) and the system is geared for the achievement of this status. It must be added, however, that there is an implicit hierarchical order which allocates higher status to the older fazendeiro who fostered the younger man in becoming a fazendeiro, regardless of the relative material wealth of either man.

While the cattle ranching economy of Roraima has survived for nearly 200 years in spite of the many factors which militate against it, Dr. Rivière envisions some abrupt changes in the near future. When the new road is completed and land is no longer in unlimited supply, the cowboys will be paid in wages instead of cattle. And this will mean the destruction of the egalitarian attitudes which underlie the present unique system.

GEORGE AND LOUISE SPINDLER
General Editors

Acknowledgments

The research on which this study is based was financed by a grant from the Ford Foundation, for which I wish to express my due thanks. I am also extremely grateful to Dr. Rodney Needham, Dr. Roberto Da Matta, and my wife, all of whom read the typescript and offered material and stylistic emendations.

PETER RIVIÈRE

Contents

THE FORGOTTEN FRONTIER

Ranchers of North Brazil

Introduction

Cowboys have been left to Hollywood and anthropologists have devoted scant attention to the ranching communities of the New World. The pastoral and nomadic peoples of the Old World have been the subject of numerous field monographs, but as Arnold Strickon, one of the few anthropologists to work on a modern Western ranching community, has noted, studies of these people in the New World are virtually nonexistent. Strickon's study of a community of the highly developed Argentinian cattle industry led him to compare it with the cattle industries of Australia and North America. He reached the conclusion that the money market is one of the most important factors determining the character of the ranching business (1965). Without denying the market-oriented character of the ranching industry throughout much of the New World, it is necessary to remember that ranching has often been a frontier occupation, carried on in regions that lacked access to markets. This study is concerned with just such a frontier community: with a people who rely almost entirely on cattle for their livelihood and who, while exhibiting many traits of the Euro-American ranching complex, cannot be said to be primarily market-oriented. Indeed it would be difficult to understand the actions and ideals of these people solely in economic terms.

The Roraimaenses, who inhabit an area of savanna grassland along Brazil's northernmost boundary, possess a socioeconomic organization that can be seen to be the result of a certain combination of historical, geographical, and environmental factors. It is the object of this case study to describe and explain the interplay among these various factors and between them and the social organization and value system of the community. I do not claim that this area exhibits unique qualities and institutions, and readers with a knowledge of frontier conditions in other areas will have no trouble in recognizing conditions and values of which they are already aware. Indeed, such values as egalitarianism and such qualities as individual initiative, traditionally associated with the American frontier, also abound here. The·socioeconomic organization found in this northern region of

1

Brazil once existed in very similar form in central Brazil. What makes this community different from similar ones in other areas is that here the isolation of the frontier region, normally a short-lived condition, has endured for a long time. Because of this the various frontier phenomena have hardened into institutionalized forms of social organization and values. Roraima is a fossilized frontier, although in order to be fair to the people of the region it must be admitted that change, as a result of both internal and external factors, is coming fast to the area. However, in this study the concentration is on the traditional system; consideration of the changes that are occurring is mainly restricted to the final chapter.

The object of this study is to demonstrate the relationship between a set of historical, geographical, and environmental factors and a particular form of socioeconomic organization, but at the same time I hope to give the reader a good idea of what the ranching life on the savannas of Roraima is like. The historical, geographical, and environmental background is provided in the first two chapters. In Chapters 3 and 4 a brief description of the present socioeconomic organization and demography of the whole territory is given. The main part of the study starts in Chapter 5 and continues until Chapter 12. These chapters cover numerous aspects of the cattlemen's lives—life on the ranch and in the cowtown, daily and annual routines, the life cycle, family and kinship, the socioeconomic organization, and the celebration of a religious festival. The theme running through these chapters is the interrelationship of environment, socioeconomic organization, and social values and attitudes. In the final chapter an attempt is made to synthesize these elements and to show how they form an obstacle to the development of the region. In this final chapter are also considered the changes that are occurring in Roraima and the factors that are bringing them about.

One point not dealt with in the text concerns the classification of the ranching people of Roraima. Discussion of this point has been purposely avoided, firstly because these people do not readily fall into any of the usual categories that have been proposed for the rural communities of Latin America, and secondly because I have reservations about the value of such classifications. Certainly the Roraimaenses are not the rural proletariat that Strickon regards cowhands as being (1965, p. 241). There are laborers in the region who could be defined thus, but they are mainly nontribal Amerindians who perform most of the manual work and who are marginal to the ranching industry. Wagley and Harris (1955, p. 436) have suggested that livestock ranches must be regarded as a subtype of the plantation subculture. Although such a classification may be generally valid in Latin America, it will not do in Roraima, where the cowhand seems to have little in common with the wage-earning plantation laborer. If the Roraimaenses are not a rural proletariat, are they then a type of peasant? Not according to either Firth (1956) or Wolf (1955), both of whom insist on a primary dependence on cultivation in their definitions of peasant. Wolf even expressly excludes livestock keepers. On the other hand, if one follows Foster (1965) and defines peasants as those who hold the concept of the limited good, then the ranching people of Roraima are peasants. And Belshaw's definition of peasant societies as "ways of life which are traditionally oriented, linked with but separate from urban centers, combining market activity with subsistence production" (1965, p. 54) certainly covers the ranchers and cowhands of Roraima. However, is it reasonable to describe as a peasant a man who, if his assets were realizable, would be worth about half a million U.S. dollars? Furthermore, since, as it will be shown, there is neither a socioeconomic nor a cultural break beween the meanest cowboy and the richest rancher and since there is considerable mobility between these two extremes, one cannot define the poorest as a peasant and the richest as something else without introducing some purely arbitrary standard by which to make a distinction that would, anyhow, be a distortion of the situation. Because of this and because, even if the Roraimaenses could be fitted into one of the existing categories, it would not help to describe them, the subject has been left out. For the sake of brevity and because of the need to have some simple label by which to refer to these people, I have chosen the term "subsistence ranchers." I am perfectly well aware that this term is inadequate, if only because there is no one in the area who owns cattle who does not sell a few from time to time, but as a description it does draw immediate attention to one of the most outstanding features of the region's socioeconomic organization. The degree to which these people live directly off their cattle almost parallels that found among the pastoralists and nomads of the Old World, although one should note at the same time that their attitudes toward and treatment of their animals are very different.

Fieldwork Problems

My first acquaintance with Roraima was in 1957, when, after three months on the Rupununi savannas of British Guiana, I crossed the frontier and traveled through the region on my way south to Manaus. I returned in June 1967 and stayed there until December 1967. This study is mainly based on this second visit.

My previous fieldwork experiences had been among South American Indians, in particular the Trio, tropical forest cultivators of the Brazil/Surinam frontier, and the fieldwork conditions that I met in Roraima were as strikingly different as the conventional contrast between Indians and cowboys. The differences are of some methodological interest, and one of them involves more than the obvious difficulty about where to draw the boundaries of one's study. The Trio are a small, self-contained group whose contact with non-Amerindian people has been very slight; it was possible to identify and isolate such influences. However, in Roraima, decisions affecting the well-being of the ranchers are made by the remote federal government in Brasilia. Furthermore, Trio culture is not simply bounded but intact and the Indians had great pride in it, so that informants were only too happy to tell me the way things are and ought to be. The average inhabitant of Roraima is perfectly well aware of his lowly place in the national order of things and is none too proud of it. The Roraimaenses always assumed that I knew better than they did, so they would never correct me; it was rarely possible to get information by making deliberate mistakes. Outright questioning of an informant usually resulted in my being told what the informant thought I ought to hear (which frequently bore a strong resemblance to what he had heard on the radio) and not what he himself thought. Accordingly, the most reliable method of collecting information was by listening to other people's conversations and afterwards asking discreet questions about the part of it that I did not understand.

There were, however, certain practical difficulties in such an approach. These resulted from the nature of the settlement pattern in the area, which consists of isolated ranches that normally house a single nuclear family. To all intents and purposes this reduces the number of informants at any ranch to one, the father, since his sons, even if full-grown, would nearly always refer me to their father when a question was directed at them. It was unthinkable that I should spend any time talking to the women, even if they had been willing to do so. On one particularly depressing occasion I found myself trapped at a ranch for a week, for almost as soon as I arrived the rancher took off, leaving me for several days with his eldest son, aged eighteen, some younger boys, his wife, and his young daughters. On the other hand, even when there were several informants available, a stay of two weeks in any one place seemed to be the limit to which one could strain the traditional hospitality.

This traditional hospitality, whereby any traveler can expect free board and lodging at any ranch house, although limiting the length of my stay, did allow me to visit almost anywhere and part of the fieldwork period was spent riding the "grubline." During this time I traveled by airplane, boat, canoe, jeep, and horse, the last always proving the most successful in giving me a feel for the country and fitting me into the scenery. After a while, mainly for reasons given above, I gave up this practice and settled in a small cowtown which is the focal center of a large ranching area. This decision proved right: not only was it easy to visit outlying ranches, but, as the entrepôt for the district, the town attracted a constant stream of visitors. In this township I lived in one of the little shops-cum-bar that, as a meeting place for everyone, proved an ideal place for my work. Those who lived in the township and those who were visiting frequently had little more to do than to talk (indeed many visitors came into town for this express purpose), and the bar was the center of gossip and animated conversation, proving, from my point of view, a trap for informants whose wariness was often reduced by a few shots of *cachaça*, the local rum. The main difficulty, since I was invariably included in the general invitations to take a drink, is obvious.

Because of the nature of the fieldwork, there was no one whom I can regard as a main informant. There were a number of people whom I came to know well and whom I found informative. Their views naturally figure prominently in this work, but because there were a number of them, I will not attempt thumbnail sketches of them at this point but rather will allow their characters to emerge from the following pages.

The language of the fieldwork was Portuguese, spoken with the strong accent of north Brazil. A few people who had picked up a smattering of English during visits to Guyana insisted on conversing in that language, as did some Amerindians who had been brought up on that side of the frontier. One or two other acquaintances spoke fluent English (better than my Portuguese), but they lived in the single urban center of the region, where I spent very little time, and the hours spent conversing with them were very few. I tended to turn to them for help when faced with a local expression or colloquialism of which I could make no sense.

I have followed convention and changed the names of people and places to which I refer, but because of the nature of the area and its small population this will barely provide an obstacle to identification. I must, therefore, ask the reader to share this convention and, even if the opportunity occurred, not to peer beneath the fragile disguises.

1

The Environment

The Território Federal de Roraima occupies the northernmost part of Brazil, stretching between the latitudes of 1 degree 30 minutes south and over 5 degrees north and the longitudes of 59 degrees west to almost 65 degrees west. Its total area is 88,000 square miles, about the size of the state of Utah. To the north and west lies Venezuela, to the east Guyana and the Brazilian state of Pará, and to the southeast, south, and southwest the state of Amazonas, of which Roraima once formed part.

The territory is dominated by the Rio Branco, a major left-bank tributary of the Rio Negro, which, in its turn, flows into the Amazon just below the city of Manaus. This river, which takes its name from the whitish color of its waters (particularly noticeable when contrasted with the humus-stained flow of the Rio Negro), is only referred to as the Rio Branco for the length of its north/south course, which ends at about 3 degrees north latitude. At this point the river divides into two major tributaries. The right-bank or western tributary, sometimes called the Rio Branco but more usually the Uraricoera, has its source in the Serra Parima, the western frontier between Brazil and Venezuela and the watershed between the Amazon and Orinoco river systems. From there the mainstream flows eastward parallel with the Serra Pacaraima to the north, a continuation of the Brazil/Venezuela frontier and of the divide between the Amazon and Orinoco basins, from which the branch receives its main tributaries.

The other main tributary, which together with the Uraricoera forms the Rio Branco, is the Takutu. In its upper and middle reaches this river flows northward and represents the frontier between Brazil and Guyana. Then, about 60 miles from its junction with the Uraricoera, it turns through a wide loop and flows southwestward. At the point where it changes course it is joined by the southward-flowing Maú, along whose course the frontier then continues. In this area, and even more so along the middle stretches of the Takutu, the watershed between the Amazonian and Guyanese river systems is very flat; the streams that feed the two river systems are intermingled and in the wet season draw their waters from the same parts of the inundated savannas.

7

The Rio Branco provides some unification for the territory, which in all other aspects is divided into three distinct zones. In geomorphological terms these consist of the lower Rio Branco, which is part of the sedimentary basin of the Amazon; of the upper part of the Rio Branco and along the main courses of the Takutu and Uraricoera, which is the worn-down peneplain of the Guiana Highlands, and of the mountainous region along the western and northern frontiers. The average height of the mountains is about 3,000 feet but they reach their highest elevation in Mt. Roraima at 9,000 feet, of which the last 1,500 feet is a vertical wall of black rock. This mountain, which stands at the trijunction of Brazil, Guyana, and Venezuela, and its description by earlier explorers gave Conan

The flat savannah (lavrado) *in the region of the middle Uraricoera.*

Doyle the idea that formed the basis of his *Lost World.* The peneplain region has an average height of 300 feet above sea level and large areas of it are flat or only gently undulating. However, one is rarely out of sight of one of the numerous ranges of small hills or isolated blocks of mountains that, as remnants of an earlier level of the Guiana Highlands, lie scattered across the whole region. These remnants are more frequent to the north, where they can be seen as outliers of the more continuous mountain ranges, with which they share numerous features; some being bare rock, others wooded, some straight-sided, and others gently rounded.

The distinction of these three zones on a geomorphological basis is further evinced by differences in vegetation and climate. The southernmost part of the territory belongs in terms of vegetation, climate, and economy to the Amazon basin. The rainfall is that of an equatorial regime, the vegetation is a thick tropical forest, and the economy is based on the extraction of forest products—wood, Brazil nuts, and rubber. The population density is extremely low and away from the main river the whole forest is virtually deserted except for Amerindians, the majority of whom remain, if not uncontacted, at least undisturbed. Many of these remarks also apply to the mountainous region in the northwest of the territory, to the Serra Parima, and to the western end of the Serra Pacaraima. This area is little known, forest-covered, and sparsely inhabited by tribal Indians. This study is concerned not with this region, but with the northeastern part of the territory, the eastern half of the Serra Pacaraima, and a 10,000-square-mile area of savanna that is more or less coincident with the peneplain and is the result of geological and climatic accident.

The character of this grassland does not remain constant throughout. The central part, which lies on either side of the Rio Branco and its two main tributaries and which is locally known as the *lavrado*, is the flattest part. Here the savanna is crisscrossed by small streams whose courses are marked by lines of *buriti* palms. The major river courses are fringed with gallery forest, often of some width, and the ranges of low hills already mentioned further serve to break the skyline. The nature of this area changes abruptly with the seasons. The streams, which during the dry season contain only a small trickle of water, become

On the edge of the mountainous region close to the Venezuelan frontier.

raging torrents in the wet season and vast areas of the savanna become inundated. Toward the south, away from this central part, larger patches of forest are to be found, giving a savanna-parkland form of scenery. The forest predominates more and more until it gradually blends into the forest of the Amazonian basin. To the north the land becomes more undulating and rocky and the number of hills, outliers of the main mountain range, increases. Tongues of grassland follow the valleys deep into the mountains, while in some areas, particularly in the region of the Rio Maú, fair-sized stretches of grassland are found on the slopes of the mountains.

Soils everywhere tend to be infertile and to suffer from alternate excesses of drought and flooding. The natural grasses are of poor nutritional quality and are not helped by the practice of burning the vegetation cover in order to encourage the growth of new, tender, green shoots, because this results in the retention of the tougher, more fire-resistant species. In the mountainous region and toward the forest edge the grasses tend to be richer, seemingly as a result of a more evenly distributed rainfall regime.

Rainfall, indeed, is the key to a number of aspects of Roraima life and economy. There are fairly well-defined wet and dry seasons. The wet season lasts from April to August during which time nearly four-fifths of the annual total of 62 inches of rain falls. However, this average obscures the fact that there is a wide variation in both quantity and distribution. This is particularly so in the dry season, which may either be quite wet or last for several months without a drop of rain falling. The wet season is the coolest time of year, but the average temperature during the coldest months (June and July, 26 degrees centigrade) is only 2.8 degrees below that for the hottest month (November). The diurnal range is much greater than the annual one, particularly during the dry season, when the temperature varies by as much as 10 degrees centigrade. The dry season climate is pleasant, although the fierceness of the midday sun is uncomfortable—especially on the savanna, where the only shade is the circle beneath the wide brim of one's hat. The relative humidity is low, the nights are cool, and the heat of the day is often ameliorated by a stiff breeze blowing from the east. During the wet season the continuous cloud cover keeps the daytime temperature down and prevents nighttime radiation cooling, but the very high relative humidity makes it an unpleasant time of year and the discomfort is greatly worsened by the swarms of blood-sucking insects that appear with the rains.

As has been mentioned above, rainfall has an important bearing on the life of Roraima. Some of these influences will be considered in greater detail in later chapters, but a brief idea of its effects will be outlined here. The intensity of social life varies enormously between wet and dry seasons. Travel across the savanna during the wet season is unpleasant and difficult. The jeeps and trucks that drive anywhere in the dry season are useless in the wet season, except on the few miles of all-weather road, and even these are often rendered impassable during particularly wet periods. At this time of year the best and surest way of traveling is by horse and movement tends to be limited to driving the cattle down to embarkation points on the main rivers. When land travel becomes more difficult, river travel becomes easier, and vice versa: a combination of factors that has influenced the economic development of the territory.

The Rio Branco would appear to offer a marvelous line of communication between Roraima and the rest of Brazil. Indeed it does, but for only a brief period of the year. Between the wet and dry seasons there is a huge variation in water level; only at the period of high water, about five months of the year, is the Rio Branco a usable waterway. In fact, the situation is worse than this, because at the point where the river leaves the peneplain for the Amazonian floodplain there are a series of rapids known as Bem Querer. These effectively prevent the largest boats from reaching the economically important savanna region except at the time of very highest flood, and mean that all people and goods have to change boats below the rapids. The effect of these factors on Roraima will be discussed more fully in Chapter 3; here it is simply intended to stress the geographical nature of the problem that the territory faces.

2

The History

The date of the initial exploration of the Rio Branco by Europeans is in doubt. The first recorded Portuguese expeditions entered the river from the Rio Negro during the late seventeenth century, but there may have been visits to the region earlier than this. It is claimed that the Dutch from Guyana arrived overland at the Rio Branco and descended it to the Rio Negro during the early decades of the same century. Official interest in the river dates from 1750 and resulted from two problems that faced the Portuguese colonists during the eighteenth century: the expansionist threats of the surrounding colonial powers—the Dutch, English, and Spanish—and the shortage of food. In 1751–1752 the king of Portugal was petitioned to grant permission for the construction of a fort on the banks of the Rio Branco in order to prevent Dutch intrusion down that river. This permission was given in 1752, but in the following year the local governor suggested that a regular patrol of the river from the nearest existing fort (on the Rio Negro) would provide adequate defense. However, the royal order was never rescinded and in 1755 the governor of Grão-Pará excused the delay in the construction of the fort, pleading lack of supplies. Although by 1762 there were settlements along the lower reaches of the Rio Branco (placed there to exploit the turtles in which the river abounded), there was still no fort. The governor of the Rio Negro reiterated the need for a fort to keep the Dutch at bay and drew attention to the advantages the Rio Branco area offered for the development of plantations and the rearing of cattle. Two years later, another report repeated that the area offered great opportunities for the rearing of cattle and that it was only idleness that prevented the start of the industry and prolonged the shortage of meat from which the Rio Negro colonists suffered. This same report referred to the earlier intention to build a fort, and stated that although the previously selected site was unknown, new knowledge indicated that the best place for it would be at the junction of the Uraricoera and the Takutu, a position that would prevent intruders coming from east or west.

This mention of a potential attack from the west is the first hint of possible trouble from the Spanish in Venezuela. This fear is more explicitly stated in an order of 1765, in which the governor of Grão-Pará ordered renewed patrolling of the Rio Branco with special attention to the western tributaries, but not the eastern ones, since the Dutch no longer represented a threat. However, when the Spanish invasion did materialize (it was a small expedition in search of El Dorado), it was not the Portuguese patrols who discovered its presence, but a Dutchman who traveled from Guyana down the Rio Branco in 1775. The Portuguese force despatched to deal with the Spaniards had little trouble in capturing the small expedition, but this minor action was important insofar as the much-discussed fort of the Rio Branco became a reality as a result of it.

The commander of the Portuguese force was ordered to construct a fort, and in his report of January 1, 1776 there is reference to the existence of such a construction on the left bank of the Rio Branco, covering the mouths of the Uraricoera and Takutu rivers. This first permanent settlement in the middle of the savanna region brought renewed interest in the cattle-rearing potential of the area; members of various expeditions that visited it were enthusiastic about the quality of the country, describing it as being like the lands of Europe that would produce both grain and wine. However, it was quickly discovered that the soil was not as fertile as the vegetation cover suggested and the garrison of Fort São Joaquim, as it came to be called, was permanently short of food, its pay in arrears, and its relief overdue. For the fifteen years following the foundation of this fort the main concern was with the Amerindian population of the area and with attempts to settle it in various permanent villages within easy reach of the fort. These attempts consistently failed, and, following a revolt in 1790 in which some Portuguese soldiers were killed, many of the Indians were deported to the lower reaches of the Rio Branco or to settlements on the Rio Negro. The remainder fled, leaving the environs of the Rio Branco denuded of its indigenous population.

The first cattle arrived on the savannas in 1787, and the first horses a little later, in 1789. The animals were regarded as extremely valuable and in the 1790 Amerindian revolt the commander of São Joaquim was told to guard the cattle well. The Crown, which held title to the land, also reserved for itself the right to ranch on it, and private settlers were not allowed to rear cattle. This, at least, was the situation on paper, but from the outset there seem to have been privately owned cattle on the Rio Branco grasslands. In 1798 a Portuguese traveler's account refers to three small ranches that existed in the region, one belonging to the Crown and the other two in private hands. This is probably wrong, since the first three ranches of the area—São Luis, São Bento, and São Marcos—were all Crown property, but it is quite possible that the traveler was misled by the large number of privately owned cattle running on Crown lands. These three ranches, which formed the foundation of the territory's cattle industry, occupied the vast tracts of land separated by the riverine boundaries of the Rio Branco, the Takutu, and the Uraricoera. Of these three ranches, only one, São Marcos, which occupies the land in the fork between the Uraricoera and the Takutu, still exists today. From 1917 to 1968 it was run by the Indian Protection Service; it has now been taken over by the Foundation for Indian Assistance (FUNAI). The other two ranches disappeared before the end of the nineteenth century, their lands divided into a large number of private holdings, mainly by squatters' rights.

Although it is not known how many head of cattle were brought originally to the savanna region, there seems to be no doubt that they bred well. Eleven years after their introduction the above-mentioned traveler estimated that there were 900–1,000 head of cattle in the region. However, this same man expressed the first words of doubt about the ranching potential of the savanna, observing that they lacked shade and, for much of the year, water also.

Following the burst of activity that saw the foundation of the first settlement, the settling of the Indian problem, and the start of the ranching industry, interest in the region declined. Apart from brief accounts by the occasional traveler (such as the English explorer Charles Waterton), the area became a backwater. Many of the Portuguese who wrote of the area appear not to have visited it; one such was André Fernandes de Souza, whose geographical and historical account (1822) of the region seems to be based on hearsay. He went out of his way to refute any idea that the savannas were unsuitable for cattle, describing the herds of the Rio Branco as the heaviest, best-fed, and fastest-multiplying in the whole of Amazonia. He also mentioned that many of the cattle had roamed and become wild, so that even the Dutch came to kill them. In fact Guyana had been a British possession since 1803, but this remark does underline the Brazilian sensitivity about this frontier, which has never been demarcated to the satisfaction of all parties. The first incident in the border dispute with Britain resulted from the ejection of a British missionary who, it was claimed, had set up his post in Brazilian territory. The British answer was to send a party of redcoats to reinstate the missionary. The incident ended without bloodshed, although not before Sir Robert Schomburgk, exploring the region under the auspices of the British government, had suggested to the Brazilian commander of Fort São Joaquim that his intransigence might result in a gunboat being sent to bombard Rio de Janeiro.

Following the formation of the State of Amazonas in 1856, of which, at that time, the present territory of Roraima formed part, there was renewed interest in the cattle-rearing potential of the savannas and some effort was made to find a way of circumventing the rapids of Bem Querer. In 1858 it was decreed that the place above the falls, called Bôa Vista, was to be the center of the district, although it would appear that it was some years after the decree before any settlement sprang up at Bôa Vista. When the French explorer Henri Coudreau visited the territory in 1884–1885, the township of Bôa Vista consisted of only twenty houses.

Although Coudreau is notoriously unreliable as an ethnographer of Amerindians his account of Roraima (1887) presents a very creditable description of the conditions in the area. He estimated the civilized population to be about 1,000 people. As well as the twenty houses, Bôa Vista had a primary school and a church under construction. The garrison of Fort São Joaquim had shrunk to a sergeant and four men, and the fort itself was in terrible condition, being flooded in the wet season and overrun with fire ants in the dry season. As well as the government-owned ranches there were thirty-two private establishments. Coudreau reckons there to have been 20,000 head of cattle, plus another 10,000 that were wild and could only be hunted, and 4,000 horses. Each year 800 head of cattle were sold down river to Manaus, and Coudreau's description of river transport at this time is particularly interesting. The cattle boats carried 10–30 head of cattle and a crew of ten. In the wet season it took ten days to descend the river, propelling the boat by oars; in the dry season it took twenty days, using a barge pole. A barge pole was also used for ascending the river during the dry season, when the journey took forty days. In the wet season the journey took sixty days and, because of the strength of the current, the boat had to be pulled up with a rope and hook. The technique in this method was for a canoe to take the hook connected to the rope and secure it to a tree. The boat was then pulled up to the hook and made fast, while the canoe took the hook forward again. However, it was just at the period of Coudreau's visit that steam launches, which could complete the journey in a tenth of the time, began to make their appearance on the Rio Branco. The Frenchman records that the main topic of conversation among the ranchers was how to circumvent the Rio Branco rapids and also notes that through their own improvidence and unwillingness to grow crops they were frequently half-starved. Both these comments remain partially true today.

During the next half-century the herds of the Rio Branco multiplied at an extraordinary rate. By 1906 there were estimated to be nearing 100,000 head, ten years after that 200,000, with 6,000 head a year being shipped down river to Manaus. By the 1930's the figure was estimated at 300,000 head. The difficulty is to know how reliable these figures are; with the exception of the last one, they are taken from the official statistics, but if they are assumed to be correct it is then necessary to account for an equally abrupt decline in the size of the herds after the 1930s. The official statistics for 1948 and 1949 give a figure of 130,000 head of cattle; not until 1964 was a figure in excess of 200,000 again given. Disregarding the exact figures, it does seem that between 1935 and 1945 the size of the Roraima herds was reduced very sharply. There are two possible causes for this decrease: one was a particularly severe epidemic of rabies (*raiva*) and the other was the discovery of diamonds in the region and the desertion of the ranches while the cattlemen became miners. These causes may have operated together so that the losses from rabies encouraged ranchers to search for diamonds.

The human population failed to increase at the same dramatic rate as the bovine one. The northern region of the territory had been created a *município* with Bôa Vista as its capital in 1890, but in 1916 a Brazilian lawyer (Luciano Pereira, 1917) visiting the region placed the population of the town at 500 souls. Decrying the lack of urban development in Amazonia, Pereira judged that its absence in Roraima sprang from absentee landlordism on the part of the large ranchers and poverty on the part of the small ones, who could not afford to maintain a town house as well as a ranch. From 1890 until the 1930s, the period during which the growth rate of the cattle herds was greatest, there was a period of upheaval in Roraima in which two factions killed each other's men and burned their ranches. Although the violence is now a thing of the past, the existence of these factions can still be seen to linger on in the social and political life of the territory. I do not intend, however, to include a discussion of these factions in this study, because their activities only slightly impinge on the everyday life of the ranching community.

By a law of 1943, what is now Roraima was separated from the State of Amazonas and created the Federal Territory of Rio Branco. This law was aimed at bringing under the direct control of the federal government regions that were particularly backward and underdeveloped. In 1964 the name of the territory was changed to Roraima for the ostensible reason that its original name caused confusion with Rio Branco, the capital city of Acre, another federal territory. The most important changes that have resulted from the creation of the territory will be described in the next chapter. An important event that occurred before the territory was created, but of which the full effects were only felt after, was the discovery of diamonds in 1938. Small deposits of gold had been found some twelve years earlier, but its extraction has never been an important economic activity in the region. Diamond mining, however, has been and still is important. In 1943 the mineral production of the territory represented nearly 60 percent of its total production, and virtually the whole of this was in diamonds. The importance of diamonds has declined and now represents less than 10 percent of the exports of the territory. One should note that the period in which diamonds achieved their greatest importance coincided with the years in which the cattle herds reached their smallest size, an estimated 118,000 head in 1943. As has been mentioned, some Brazilian commentators have seen a direct connection between these facts, claiming that the ranchers abandoned their cattle and went in search of diamonds. However, the long-term effect on the region has been the attraction of diamond hunters from other areas of Brazil, thus helping to swell the rapid increase in population that followed the creation of the territory.

Compared with the previous century and a half, the population of Roraima has risen very sharply in the last thirty years. The total population, corrected for the boundaries adjusted at the time the territory was created, was 12,130. By 1950 this figure had risen to 18,116, and in 1960 to 29,486. I am of the opinion that the 1970 census figures will show a decline in the growth rate of the two earlier decades, because certain of the causes for expansion have now ceased to operate. In particular, it has been realized that the diamond mining does not provide the rich rewards originally expected. Also, many of the people who came to the area during the 1950s came to fill the newly-created bureaucratic posts that became available with the establishment of the new federal territory. These facts reveal themselves to some extent in the distribution of the population. Firstly, although the population density of the whole territory remains very low, that of the southern part, the Município of Caracaraí (all of which lies in the Amazonian forest) is one of the lowest in the whole of Brazil, less than .01 people per square mile. This represents a total population of 3,318, of which about 1,000 live in the municipal capital, Caracaraí, the second largest settlement in the territory. The remainder of the population, 26,168 people, live in the municipal region of Bôa Vista, which includes the ranching, diamond-mining, and administrative centers. Even so, the population density here is only .1 per square mile.

Secondly, the ratio of urban to rural population has undergone a very rapid change. In 1940 Bôa Vista had a population of 1,398 and the next largest settlement was Catrimâni with 162 people. By 1950 the population of the town of Bôa Vista had grown to 5,132. By 1960 it was 11,785, nearly 45 percent of the population of the municipal region. It seems likely that this move to the town has continued and that about half the population of the territory now lives in urban areas. Except for the second largest settlement in the territory, Caracaraí, which has already been mentioned, the only other places that could be regarded as nucleated settlements have fewer than 200 residents. The remainder of the population lives in scattered ranches on the savannas.

As will be seen in the next chapter, Bôa Vista, as the main center of population and the administrative, economic, commercial, educational, and ecclesiastical capital, dominates the territory. There is, however, one further comment that should be made at this point; the population figure for Bôa Vista is slightly unreal, because many families have ranches on the savannas as well as houses in town but, for prestige reasons, prefer to list themselves as urban dwellers. The reason for the growth of Bôa Vista is tied to the list of functions just mentioned, but one might add that its growth has been made possible by greatly improved communications both within and without the region. A consideration of this topic opens the next chapter.

3

Roraima Today

In this chapter and the next the reader will be given a description of Roraima as it is today. It is not intended that this should be an exhaustive or analytic account of the social, economic, and political institutions of the territory, but rather that it should provide a setting against which the treatment of the ranching industry may be arranged and understood. The topics dealt with in this chapter are communications, the economic structure, education, medical services, and the church.

Communication and Transport

Communications and the cost of transport both within and without the territory are key factors in understanding the region. As has already been pointed out, the Rio Branco is not the useful waterway that it might appear to be from the map. The reason for this is its great variation in water level, a situation worsened by the presence of a stretch of rapids just downstream from the savanna region, which renders it useless as a navigable waterway throughout much of the year. Even so, the river, as it has been in the past, remains the economic lifeline between Roraima and the rest of Brazil. A description of river travel in the last century was given in the last chapter and, since cattle are the most important commodity transported by river today, a description of modern practices will be reserved for Chapter 7. However, one may note at this point that as well as the cattle that go downstream almost all goods that are used in the territory have to come upstream. The high cost of living, especially for imported items, reflects this situation. The cost of river transport from Manaus to Caracaraí is .1 new cruzeiro (*cruzeiros novas* or NCr$) per kilo, to which must be added a further NCr$ .02 a kilo for road transport from Caracaraí to Boa Vista. This means, for example, that a bottle of beer that costs NCr$ 1 in Manaus costs NCr$ 2 in Boa Vista. As well as the high prices, the periodicity of the river transport means that there is frequently a shortage of many goods, including such essential commodities as wheat, sugar, salt, coffee, gasoline, and kerosene. In the past there have been times, especially in years of low rainfall and a drawn-out dry season, in which the lack of basic subsistence foods has become serious.

Until 1945 the river was the only means of access for both people and goods coming from other parts of Brazil, but from that date there has been a regular commercial air service between Bôa Vista and Manaus. This service, operated with a DC-3, consists of six round trips a week and on one day the flight is extended to a round trip to Georgetown, the capital of Guyana. The runway at Bôa Vista has recently been tarmacadamed in anticipation of a jet flight service. The air service, operated by one of Brazil's most prominent airlines, is efficient and reliable, but the high cost of air freight tends to limit its use to passengers and goods with a high cost-to-weight ratio. All flights are well filled and this service has had an inestimable effect in introducing new ideas to the territory and widening the horizons of the Roraimaense, who now goes to spend weekends in Manaus and holidays in Rio de Janeiro or São Paulo, which are less than twenty-four hours away.

Besides the commercial service, the Brazilian Air Force (FAB) has fairly frequent flights in and out of the territory, and once a month an aircraft visits four other places in the region as well as Bôa Vista. Space on these flights is mainly taken up by passengers who travel free of charge—almost everyone is eligible for a free flight, but a certain amount of string-pulling is necessary to ensure space for oneself. Furthermore, because FAB planes do not keep to a schedule, those who can afford it normally take the commercial line in order to save delays. But it would be impossible to overestimate the importance of FAB in opening up the interior of Brazil, and their aircraft, late or not, are for many isolated communities the single link with civilization.

Within the territory itself there are a number of small charter companies operating with single-engined aircraft. Most people who can afford it now travel into the interior by this means, and all the aircraft are kept very busy ferrying passengers and goods to ranches and diamond workings. Most ranches of any size have their own airstrip, even if it is rarely used more than once a year. As well as the small charter companies, both the Roman Catholic Church and the American Protestant missionaries operate small aircraft, which will normally carry people and goods if they have room. The development of this internal air service has made a big difference to the life of the ranching community and the diamond prospectors (*garimpeiros*), because now no part of the savanna and no diamond working are more than two hours from Bôa Vista and at any time of year.

Roraima has no land connection with the rest of Brazil. There has been much discussion for a long time about a road or rail link with Manaus. Indeed, between 1893 and 1895 an exploratory trail was cut between Manaus and Bôa Vista, but nothing came of it. With the recent increase in road building in Brazil the possibility of a road joining Roraima with the rest of Brazil is greatly enhanced. The construction of such a road began, at the Manaus end, in 1968; the plans include a road running east from Bôa Vista into Guyana and another north into Venezuela, where it will connect with the Pan-American highway system. At the moment the total number of miles of road that are regarded as suitable for all-weather usage is less than 300. While the main stretch is that connecting Bôa Vista with Caracaraí, there are two other lengths; one runs northwest from Bôa Vista, then divides with one fork going to the middle reaches of the Uraricoera and the other to the agricultural colony of Taiano, and the other length goes from the east bank of the Rio Branco opposite Bôa Vista to Bom Fim on the Guyana border. Although all these stretches of road are regarded as suitable for all-weather use, they are often impassable following periods of heavy rain. Besides these stretches of road a network of jeep trails runs everywhere across the savanna, but these trails are impassable throughout the wet season and even periodically during the dry season—the problem being not only unfordable streams and rivers, but also vast areas of flooded and swampy savanna.

In Bôa Vista itself there are a few saloon cars but there, as everywhere in the country, the normal vehicle is the jeep. Many of the richer ranchers have their own jeeps, and for those who do not there are jeep taxis that may be hired for local journeys in Bôa Vista or for more extensive trips onto the savanna.

The cowboy rides into town. Note the hitching post.

There are also a number of trucks in the territory, used mainly for carrying goods from Caracaraí to Bôa Vista and for bringing produce into town from the agricultural colonies. During the dry season these trucks may also be hired to carry supplies to ranches and small settlements.

Bicycles are a popular if not common form of transport, not only in the towns, but also on the savanna, where for short journeys they are preferred to horses. However, the horse, which is the traditional means of transport, has not lost its importance, and is still used by men and women for most journeys. Indeed, during the wet season, horseback remains the only feasible and reliable way of traveling. The importance of pack animals (oxen, horses, mules, or donkeys) has decreased, although they are still used where jeeps cannot go in the mountains and during the wet season. Around the ranch, the ox cart is still used for transporting such loads as corral posts and rails or firewood.

Many of these forms of transport are of relatively recent arrival in the territory; when I first visited the area in 1957 the internal air charter service was in an embryonic stage and very few motor vehicles existed in the region. The greatly improved means of communication in the area have brought considerable changes in the way of life on the savannas, the introduction of new ideas, new things, new people, and, above all, a reduction in isolation. Two other elements in the communication system have had an influence in this field. The transistor radio has replaced the large tube-type radio, which, although it existed in the region, was a relatively scarce item because its size and price and the size and price of its batteries made it impractical; the smaller transistor is free of these handicaps and few families are now without one. Coupled with this, the local

Ox-carts are still used for transport around the ranch.

radio station, Radio Roraima, gives two hours a day, one in the morning and one in the evening, to transmitting messages for its listeners and few of the savanna dwellers fail to listen to the evening session. Besides this, there are dispersed throughout the territory a number of government radio transmitters and operators, the use of which is free for all members of the public.

Bôa Vista, the Capital of Roraima

The center of the communication system in the territory is Bôa Vista, and this fact is part and parcel of the domination that this city holds on the whole life of the region. One of the most important factors in the recent rapid growth of urban population has been the development of easier travel, for it is now feasible for the rancher to move between a ranch and a town house. The advantages of living in Bôa Vista are neither immediately obvious nor accepted by everybody. The arguments against living in Boa Vista are that the cost of living is much higher there than on the savanna, (food in particular being expensive and at times in short supply—even the provision of meat in this capital of a ranching area is a matter of continual political dispute) and that the environment of the city is unhealthy, it being called the mosquito capital of the world. But these disadvantages are easily outweighed in the minds of the majority by the city's obvious advantages and attractions. Bôa Vista is the center of activity and, as such, caters to the Brazilian love of *movimento* and *zoada*—the hustle and bustle of urban life. In comparison, the quiet existence on the savanna is regarded as very *triste*.

At this point, it is worth digressing to give the reader a brief description of Bôa Vista. The city is built on a high bank on the west side of the Rio Branco. The old part of the city faces the river and has a genuinely beautiful view. The new part of the city, the plans for which were based on those of Washington, D.C. (although this fact is barely recognizable from the air and is completely obscured from the ground), lies back from the river, and one might almost say faces toward the airport, thus symbolizing the change in importance from river to air transport and links with the outside world. The center of the new part of the city consists of a large square, which depending on season is a quagmire of red mud or blowing lateritic dust. Surrounding this square are official buildings—the governor's residence, the offices of territorial and municipal administration, schools, a new cathedral in process of construction, and a hotel, formerly government-owned, but now in private hands. Between this area and the old part of the city lies the commercial center, and although very small, this is the really active part of the city. The three or four streets consist of shops, offices, and bars. Through most of the day there is a sense of busy activity, even if half the crowd is there just to watch the other half. Stretching up and down the river bank from the urban center lie the main dwelling areas, the houses for the main part being small bungalows set in their own gardens, but one does not get an impression of size and it is never obvious where the 12,000 listed inhabitants of the city live.

Besides its opportunities for meeting people and having a drink, Bôa Vista is the only place in the territory with a cinema and other organized entertainments—basketball and football leagues and concerts by visiting musicians. It has a virtual monopoly of all commercial and business activities—the only bank in the territory is there—and complete domination in the administrative and political fields. It is the center for all medical services. Although medical posts were set up at various places throughout the territory, most have ceased working. With the exception of a small missionary hospital, the only medical posts in the territory are in Bôa Vista, as are all the doctors.

Avenida Jaime Brasil, the main street of Bôa Vista.

The city is also the center of religious life, which is dominated by the Roman Catholic Church, represented in the territory by the Italian brotherhood, Missão da Consolata. The *prelazia*, a pleasant old building with high ceilings, is in the old part of the town, overlooking the river, as is the old cathedral of Nossa Senhora do Carmo. The fathers are very energetic in maintaining contact with their flock both within and without the city and in fighting off the growing influence of various Protestant sects. A large mission station near the township of Murusu incorporates a hospital, a school, and an orphanage and the church has recently started work among tribal Indian groups of the upper Câtrimani and Mucajai rivers. Contact with communities and families in other parts of the territory is maintained by traveling priests who perform the baptisms and marriages that have arisen since their last visit.

The main competition to the Roman Catholic Church comes from an American Baptist group. These missionaries concentrate their efforts on tribal Indians (an attempt to work among the civilized Indians on the savannas failed, reputedly because of the intervention of the Roman Catholic fathers), but they also have a chapel in Bôa Vista and run a school and a medical clinic, both of which are open to all comers. Other Protestant sects represented in the territory are the Jehovah's Witnesses and the Seventh Day Adventists.

One of the most important reasons for the growth of Bôa Vista is that it is the only place in the territory where education above the primary school level is available, and education has become an important goal in the ambitions of the Roraimaenses. Certainly part of the move from country to town may be accounted for by the desire for education, and it is nearly always the ostensible reason given for making the move. Those who can afford it maintain a house in Bôa Vista where their wife and children can live during the school term. This has given rise to an increase in ranches left in the care of managers, since the rancher often follows his family to town. However, the need for education cannot be entirely blamed for this and many ranchers, particularly small ones, have been attracted to Bôa Vista by the possibility of obtaining a civil service post with the territorial administration. Those who are unable or unwilling to leave the savanna can usually find a relation in the city who will look after a child during the school term and who is usually happy to do so, since he will benefit from the supply of food sent by the parents from the country where food is more plentiful and cheaper.

In the rural districts there is a relatively large number of primary schools; all nucleated settlements contain one, and out on the savanna a ranch will act as a schoolhouse for the neighborhood. However, because of the nature of the settlement pattern, access to a school is frequently difficult, particularly in the wet season, and the poorer and more isolated ranchers often make no attempt to send their children. The influence of education on the growth of nucleated settlements will be considered later.

Before turning to consider the economic structure of the territory, final emphasis on the domination of Bôa Vista over the region may be given by a brief outline of the distribution of population. The second largest town in the territory is Caracaraí, with a population of 576 in 1960. This township is the capital of the *município* that includes the whole of the lower Rio Branco, an area of more or less uninhabited tropical forest containing only two other nucleated settlements, both of less than 200 inhabitants. In the *município* of which Bôa Vista is capital there are only three other settlements of any size and even these have less than 200 inhabitants. One of them is a diamond-mining center; one, near the Guyana border, is a center for diamonds, cattle, and trade (frequently used as euphemism for smuggling); and the third is a cowtown and will be examined in detail in Chapter 11. Besides these settlements there are a number of other agglomerations of people, such as government agricultural colonies and Amerindian villages (locally known as *malocas*). The remainder of the population lives on ranches that are scattered across the savanna, often at some distance from each other.

The Economy of Roraima

The economic basis of the territory is cattle ranching. As was indicated in the last chapter, the statistics on the number of cattle in the territory are not reliable, nor are those on land holdings and other related subjects, since no cadastral survey of the territory has been made. Nonetheless, the figures from the 1960 census give some idea of the structure of the cattle industry. In that year there were estimated to be 200,000 head of cattle in the territory, distributed among 533 ranches. The size of these ranches varied considerably: 283 of them were under 1,000 hectares, 228 were between 1,001 and 5,000 hectares, 18 were between 5,001 and 10,000 hectares, and 4 were over 10,000 hectares. These figures include some very small ranches that barely deserve the title and, indeed, are not so regarded in Roraima. Most ranchers have no idea of the land size of their ranches and assessment is made in terms of number of cattle. Because of variations in quality of the pasturage, it is not possible to convert land area into number of cattle, but the average for the whole region is approximately one beast to every 80–100 acres, the density being lower on the flat *lavrado* and higher on the pastures in the mountain valleys and near the forest edge.

The average annual sale of cattle is about 11,000 head, of which approximately 8,000 are shipped to market in Manaus and the other 3,000 are consumed in the territory. This last figure probably does not include those cattle killed on ranches and in the small savanna settlements, where the consumption of meat is much higher than in Bôa Vista, and it would not be unreasonable to add another 3,000 head to the total. Even so a total production of 14,000 head on herds numbering 200,000 is only a turnover of 7 percent—a ludicrously low figure by the standards of the cattle industries of southern Brazil, Argentina, and Uruguay. A number of reasons that help account for the low production, including the use of cattle as wages, will be discussed in Chapter 10. Just one factor will be mentioned here—the availability of markets. As has already been indicated, low water in the Rio Branco prevents communication between the savanna region and its main market, Manaus, for over half the year. It is possible that the ranchers could sell more of their cattle in the territory than they do at present, but they prefer not to because the price is controlled and they can obtain a better deal by selling to Manaus. This fact has the rather curious result that, while meat is cheap in Bôa Vista, it is often very scarce and its supply is a matter of much political maneuvering. Potential markets exist in Venezuela, Guyana, and the Caribbean, but at the moment the export or import of cattle is restricted on all sides, although some animals undoubtedly get to Venezuela. However, even if there were markets for Roraima cattle, there are further questions that need to be answered. Are there cattle to sell and just how interested in a market economy is the rancher? The answer to the first part of the question is a qualified yes—meaning that there are more cattle for sale in certain years. The answer to the second part is more complicated. There are many ranchers in the area who regard their business as a commercial enterprise, but there are an equal number (they tend to be the smaller ones) who sell according to their immediate cash requirements and not according to the number of salable cattle they have. The situation is frequently made worse by the system of marketing. The rancher sells to a middleman (*marchante*), who arranges transport and sale in Manaus. The *marchante* is regarded as the rancher's friend, since in the absence of any other system of credit in the territory he will pay in advance. While this is undoubtedly a valuable service to the ranchers, it often results in the rancher overestimating his stock and in due course having to sell cattle not yet ready for market in order to cover his debts.

The second most important economic activity of the territory is mineral extraction, almost exclusively diamond mining. The total reported value of this activity is small (the total value in 1963 was NCr$ 10,570, compared with the value of cattle exported to Manaus that year, which was NCr$ 171,592) but most Roraimaenses believe that the true figure is much higher and that a large part of the production is smuggled out of the country into Venezuela and Guyana. Smuggled goods, coming from Guyana and consisting of such items as transistor radios and whisky, are sent downriver and represent a hidden income. The economic activity of the southern, forested part of the territory is mainly concerned with the extraction of natural products, balata, wood, and Brazil nuts. Hides and animal skins represent a reasonable fraction of the territory's annual income, but far less than one might expect, because the cattle leave the area alive (and thus take their hides with them), and the hides of cattle slaughtered in the region are mainly needed for local use.

There is virtually no export of agricultural produce from the territory; in some years there is a surplus of rice or manioc but this is by no means assured and just as often it is necessary to import rice into the region. In the not-so-distant past all foodstuffs, with the exception of beef and *farinha* (the flour of the manioc root), had to be imported into the territory. During the dry season, when the river was closed to transport, the Roraimaenses often faced famine. The situation is not so bad today as a result of the development of three government-sponsored agricultural colonies that were started in the 1940s and became fully operational in the 1950s. Two of these colonies were established on the forest edge along the southern boundary of the savanna, and the third on a patch of *terra roxa* (soil made famous in Brazil by the coffee plantations of São Paulo) to the northwest of Bôa Vista. Although these colonies, mainly peopled by immigrants from the northeast of Brazil and a few Japanese families, have done much to make the territory self-subsistent in necessities, no attempts have been made to employ improved farming methods; there is little machinery and the technique remains the slash-and-burn cultivation practiced by the *caboclos* and Indians of the tropical forest.

The wages of the civil servants who administer the territory represent one of its major sources of income. This large occupational group has come into existence since the territory was created in 1943. In 1967 there were 1,134 civil servants in Roraima; together with the larger ranchers they form the richest segment of the population. It is on the salaries of these people that many of the commercial businesses in Bôa Vista exist. Such businesses are mainly small; some sell just homemade soft drinks; the largest concerns deal with such items as trucks, jeeps, and gasoline; the majority fall somewhere between these two extremes and are shops that profess some degree of specialization. Thus a shop that sells clothes and cloth is unlikely to sell canned goods and hardware, nor a hardware store such items as newspapers, cheap books, cosmetics, and trinkets. There are a number of bars, some of which are also restaurants, two boardinghouses as well as the main hotel, and such services as barbers.

An outstanding feature of the territory is the total absence of any form of industry or manufacturing that is not concerned with supplying such minor local needs as bricks, tiles, and leather goods. It is particularly noticeable that the ranching industry has not given rise to any businesses concerned with the processing of animal products.

In the next chapter we will consider the people of Roraima and their social structure.

4

The People of Roraima

The growth, density, and distribution of the population of Roraima have all been described in earlier chapters, but a brief recapitulation will be provided here. From the first settlement at the end of the eighteenth century until 1940 the population grew very slowly, reaching only 12,000 by the latter date. Since then the growth rate has been very rapid with the population nearing 30,000 by 1960. This period of population increase has coincided with a rise in the proportion of urban dwellers, although almost all of these are in one city. In spite of the recent growth in population, the density remains very low and the tropical forest part of Roraima has the lowest density of any area in Brazil.

The Population Divisions

The Roraimaense of today recognizes three segments in the population of the territory. Firstly, there are the *Indios*, Amerindians living under tribal conditions well away from the main areas of population. They are mainly to be found in the headwater regions to the west of the territory, along the frontier with Venezuela. They do not figure in this study and their contact with the main part of the population is limited to missionaries and the more adventurous diamond miners, except on the rare occasions when bands of them have appeared in the vicinity of Caracaraí—an event which gives rise to great excitement and undue anxiety.

The important segment of the population in terms of both numbers and socioeconomic significance are the *brancos* or *civilizados*, as the Brazilians are locally called. Ethnically they are, like many Brazilians, a mixture of Portuguese and various other European nations, African, and Amerindian. It is impossible to identify any specific type, since physical features range through almost every possibility. There are those who claim pure Portuguese descent; their appearance—they often have blond hair and blue eyes—frequently supports them in this. The

African element is not particularly marked in the region, and those of strongly negroid cast are very few. Amerindian physical features are more common but, for reasons given below,· such an ancestry is never claimed. In Roraima, the term *branco* has nothing to do with skin color; it is a cultural description synonymous with *civilizado*, a term that conveys the sense rather better. Although the term *moreno* may be used to describe someone of obvious African descent, this word does not indicate any socioeconomic distinction. The important distinction is between *branco* or *civilizado* and *caboclo*.

The *caboclos* make up the third part of the Roraima population. The term is used throughout Brazil, but its meaning varies in different parts of the country. In Roraima, where the word is deformed to *caboco*, it means a civilized Amerindian. There are 6,000 or more *caboclos* in the territory, mainly Carib-speaking Macusi or Arawak-speaking Wapishana living in about fifty villages or *malocas*. The form of these villages varies considerably and may represent a sort of appendage to a *civilizado* township, a separate nucleated settlement, or a relatively widely dispersed collection of houses whose inhabitants regard themselves as forming an entity. These people have retained, in slightly modified form, their traditional subsistence economy—the cultivation of bitter cassava by slash-and-burn technique, and hunting and fishing—mainly the latter in this area. However, the *caboclos* are also firmly tied to the economy of the *civilizados*, since they all wear Brazilian-style clothes and seek to buy such things as *cachaça* (the local rum) and such assorted manufactured goods as clothes, plastic combs, bicycles, radio sets, and even canned food. To obtain the money for these goods, they sell their agricultural produce—mainly *farinha*—and their labor. In a general way, it is true to say that all manual labor in the territory is performed by *caboclos*, for the *civilizados* regard such work with distate unless it is concerned directly with cattle or horses.

In Roraima to refer to or address someone as *caboclo* is highly derogatory and the term carries a definite pejorative sense. In the interior the boundary between *civilizados* and *caboclos* assumes considerable importance, and the former class is constantly trying to reinforce the distinction. In some areas of behavior and outlook the boundary is quite clearly demarcated, but in others it is far less obvious. There are numerous Amerindians who have adopted a purely Brazilian way of life and who refer to less "civilized" Indians disparagingly as *caboclos*, but whose status as *civilizados* is not recognized by the members of that class. It is among these Indians, who have lost their own cultural tradition but have not gained acceptance in the new one, that the behavior that distinguishes *civilizado* from *caboclo* becomes most obvious. There is in Roraima a clear association between the *caboclo* and food seasoned with pepper, and the *civilizado* and salted food. On one occasion I observed a number of self-styled *civilizados* (all of obviously pure Amerindian descent) prefer to eat a scratch meal of salt beef and *farinha* rather than fish in a pepper stew with *beiju* (the traditional Amerindian cassava bread). While in a case such as this the Brazilian would not be so fussy about his status, there are many areas in which his attitude toward the *caboclo* finds expression, for example, in the treatment of *caboclas* (Indian women) compared with that of Brazilian women. The *cabocla* is seen as fair game for sexual adventure and is treated with an open familiarity that would be regarded as extremely offensive if used to a woman of the *civilizados* class. Such greetings as *"Está gorda?"* (Are you fat?), which are normally used between male friends, are addressed to *caboclas*. This discrimination is particularly noticeable at dances and *festas*, where, if *caboclos* are allowed to attend (and more often than not they are excluded), they do no dance with Brazilian women. On the other hand, the *caboclas* are encouraged to dance and when a dance is held in a *maloca* the young *civilizados* flock to attend. The *caboclos*, however, do have a role at *civilizados'* dances, since, as is so widely true of subordinate classes, they provide the musicians.

The main focus for more serious conflict between the *civilizados* and *caboclos* is land and property. The latter claim that the ranchers have encroached and are still encroaching on what is rightfully their land and that the cattle have displaced the animals they used to hunt. The *caboclos* also claim that cattle break into their fields and eat the crops. A typical train of events is that a *caboclo* kills a cow, using as a genuine or spurious excuse the damage that it was doing in his field. The rancher responds by a physical beating of the *caboclo*. The *caboclo* has no way to combat the physical force employed by the rancher, and has little hope for redress through legal channels, which are operated by and in the interest of the ranching community. The Indian Protection Service (now FUNAI) is represented in the territory, but to the *caboclo* it appears as a remote organization that frequently sides with the *civilizados*. The *caboclo*'s best chance is to form a *compadre* relationship with an influential *civilizado* and most *caboclos* try to do this. The *caboclos* see this as a means of having personal links with a patron who will support their case. Undoubtedly there are occasions on which it does work according to the *caboclo*'s view of the relationship, but the advantage of this ritual relationship would seem to lie more often with the *civilizado*, who can often obtain free labor by requesting help under the guise of their *compadresco* bond.

Ethnosocial Mobility

It is possible for the *caboclo* to make the complete crossing from one ethnic group to the other, but it involves the total loss of all his Indian ways and ties. The most effective way is through adoption, a system whereby a rancher adopts a young Amerindian (normally a boy) and brings him up as his son. The *filho de criação*, as the foster child is called, takes the name of his foster family. There are elements of luck in this system, for it is clear that a child is fostered by chance and not on his ability. There is also the matter of the treatment that he receives from his foster family. The system is open to great abuse and often the child ends up as an unpaid servant; one Brazilian ethnographer (Diniz, 1966) has referred to the practice of fosterage as disguised slavery. Certainly I have seen households in which the discrimination against a *filho de criação* is very marked, the foster child being made to do all the manual chores of the house, such as hauling water and cutting firewood, and to take his meals standing in the kitchen, and being bullied by even the youngest members of the family. On the other hand, there are many foster *caboclo* children who are extremely well treated and who are given the same opportunity for education and economic advancement as other members of the family; such a child grows up with his *civilizado* status assured.

Marriage is another means by which the boundary may be crossed, but this route favors *caboclas* for while unions between such women and *civilizados* are common, those between *caboclos* and *civilizadas* are extremely rare. The children of such unions take the status of *civilizado*, because they will almost certainly be brought up as such and the boundary is defined by cultural background rather than by appearance.

It is also possible for a man who grew up a *caboclo* to achieve the status of *civilizado*, at least in a local setting. The requirements here include not simply the adoption of *civilizado* ways, but also his proven ability, normally as a cowboy, so that he is accepted as an equal by the *civilizado* cowhands alongside whom he works. He will be seen in their company, eating and drinking with them, and perhaps even attending a *civilizado* dance, but whether or not he is accepted outside this peer group as a *civilizado* will depend upon the degree to which he has divorced himself from his cultural origins. One should note here that wealth, as such, provides no entry into the ranks of the *civilizados*; a few Amerindians own numerous head of cattle and are richer than many *civilizados*, but because of their cultural background they remain *caboclos*.

Socioeconomic Classes

The fundamental social division in Roraima is that between *civilizado* and *caboclo*, and in rural areas it is the only important one. It seems possible that half a century ago this was the only important distinction, since then virtually the whole population was rural and the whole of the *civilizado* part was engaged in ranching. Today, however, because of the social, economic, and political changes that have taken place, there are a number of classes among the *civilizados* that are partly based on occupational differences and that, in turn, carry different prestige ratings. The following brief account is in no way exhaustive.

The ranchers still retain their traditional position at the head of the socioeconomic hierarchy, but as a class they have lost much of their political power to the civil servants, the administrators who appeared following Roraima's designation as a federal territory. This latter class possesses considerable social status because of their white-collar government employment and their urban residence. The ranchers and civil servants are not exclusive groups; many ranchers, particularly the poorer ones, have for economic reasons entered the ranks of the civil service and many government employees have acquired ranches. However, because of their wealth and standing in the territory the traditionally powerful ranching families still hold much power without needing to join the civil service. Indeed, under the guise of modern political differences can still be seen the old factional rivalries of these families.

Another new occupational class in the territory is that of the diamond miners, the *garimpeiros*, who arrived in considerable numbers in the 1940s and

1950s. This class has a relatively low status in the eyes of the ranching and administrative classes, who regard them as unreliable, drunken, quarrelsome, and immoral. Much of the *garimpeiro's* work is with his hands, a fact that in itself is lowering. However, an abrupt transition overtakes the successful diamond miner who is able to employ others to do the manual labor. It is surprising how many successful *garimpeiros* stay in Roraima, but less surprising that nearly all that do stay buy ranches and thus achieve respectability. Even those who initially invest their good fortune in some sort of commercial enterprise invariably end up by owning a ranch. Thus one well-known case is that of the lucky miner who started what is now a thriving air charter business and in due course also bought himself a ranch. Cattle ranching is regarded as a safe if unspectacular investment and contrasts with diamond mining, which is seen as a gamble for high stakes. Diamond mining is also recognized as a suitable occupation for young men before they settle down.

Besides these three main occupational classes, there are also a number of professional and commercial men who are too few in number to form recognizable classes, but who have much in common with the administrative class, with which they overlap to a certain extent. For example, there are doctors in private practice and those employed by the government. In fact, there is considerable overlap between all the occupational classes—the example of the man who came to the territory as a civil servant but gave that up to be a diamond miner and now owns a fair-sized ranch as well is not unusual. Nor have the ranching families hesitated to enter commerce or the civil service. Even if the boundaries of these occupational classes are not rigid, each class does contain a core of people whose attitudes and expectations are clearly distinguishable from those of the other classes.

In terms of wealth and education, each of these occupational classes covers a wide spectrum. In Roraima wealth and education do not necessarily coincide and it is quite possible to have either one without the other. This is by no means an unusual occurrence in a frontier situation, but it is one that causes considerable distress among many of the urban inhabitants of Bôa Vista, particularly among the civil servants, who expect some close relationship between the standard of education and the level of wealth. Their mouthpiece is the single newspaper of the territory, the weekly *Tribuna da Norte*, which inveighs against such things as the hotel's allowing the well- and poorly-educated to mix at a dance, the untidiness caused by children's kites caught in the overhead power lines and trees, the owners of bars who do not discourage prostitutes, and the ownerless dogs whose unseemly public behavior threatens to corrupt the young. Such complaints seem unreasonable, even ludicrous, against the background of Bôa Vista in particular and Roraima in general, but they are indicative of the decline of the frontier influence and the growth of a less adventurous urban, middle-class attitude.

However, this study is concerned not with the urban population of Roraima but with the rural, ranching community, among whom the frontier characteristics of egalitarianism and equal opportunity still exist.

5

The Cattlemen

Almost everyone who lives in the savanna region of Roraima is associated in some way, either directly or indirectly, with ranching. However, not everyone who owns a few head of cattle is regarded as a rancher or *fazendeiro*. There are innumerable small holders, nearly all of whom own a few head of cattle, but who normally have some other occupation by which they eke out their existence. These occupations include such things as saddlery making and diamond mining, and these people normally cultivate crops in forest garden sites, using the slash-and-burn technique of cultivation. These small-time cattle owners are referred to as *moradores* and their places as *sitios*. The line between *fazendeiro* and *morador* is not clearly defined, but it ultimately depends on the number of cattle owned, since this is the criterion of social and economic prestige. As well as the *morador* and the *fazendeiro*, there is the *vaqueiro*, the cowhand. Although *vaqueiro* is used to mean cowhand in Roraima, it has a more specific meaning, since it is applied to only one man on each ranch. He is responsible to the rancher for the cattle, and if the work is more than he can manage it is up to him to hire and pay extra help. As will be seen below, there are many variations on this theme, but the word *vaqueiro* will be reserved throughout to apply to this position and the term cowhand will be used to refer to anyone who works cattle. It should finally be noted here that, while *fazendeiro* and *morador* are exclusive categories, the *vaqueiro* overlaps both. Many *vaqueiros* work for a rancher while they themselves have their own *sitio* or even *fazenda*. The importance of this practice will be described in Chapter 10, but it is indicative of the egalitarian ethos that pervades the region, a factor that reveals itself in many aspects of life, including dress.

Dress

The everyday clothes of the rancher and the cowhand are indistinguishable, and their appearance is far from glamorous. In spite of the fact that many of the present Roraimaenses came from the northeast of Brazil, in ascending the Amazon

Pedrão (Big Peter), a vaqueiro of Roraima.

and the Rio Branco they have left behind much of *nordestino* custom and tradition. For example, they have discarded the traditional leather clothing which, while so essential among the thorn bushes of the *caatinga*, is barely necessary on the open plains of the Rio Branco. Nearly everyone on the savanna wears loose and badly fitting trousers that have baggy legs narrowed in to the ankles. Shirts tend to be equally loose-fitting and are worn outside the trousers. Most clothes are homemade; ready-to-wear shirts and trousers are worn, but are often kept for best because they are of poor quality and do not last long if submitted to the hard wear of everyday. Everyone wears a hat, the usual type being of straw with a wide brim. Felt hats can also be bought in Bôa Vista, but these are usually kept for best by those who own them (mainly the richer ranchers), since they are hotter and heavier than the straw type. The hat is virtually a distinguishing mark of the cattleman; visitors from the town rarely wear them, and in a mixed working party of boatmen and cowhands it is always possible to pick out the latter by the presence of their hats. Few people wear shoes more elaborate than sandals with a thong that passes between the two biggest toes. Boots are occasionally worn, but most often by those who have lately come to be ranchers rather than by those who have been brought up in the ranching tradition.

No additional clothes are worn for riding. A man sometimes dons a pair of leather leggings, a vestige of the full-size chaps of the northeast. Spurs are usually worn, always if cattle are to be worked; these are often strapped on to bare feet. A leather thong riding lash hangs by a loop from the right wrist. A knife of some sort, from a small sheath knife to a long machete, is always carried when leaving the vicinity of the ranch; as many people as can afford them carry revolvers, usually a .22 caliber, but occasionally a .32, .38, or even a .45. The smaller caliber is more popular because of the price and the weight of the ammunition. Marksmanship with these guns is of a low order and they are very rarely used. Sometimes as a result of boredom an old tin is used as a target, but the only times I observed a revolver practically employed were an unsuccessful attempt to hunt a deer from horseback and the successful slaughter of a cow from point-blank range. Even if they are of little practical value, there is considerable etiquette surrounding the wearing of sidearms. No one will sit down to eat wearing a gun, nor would one enter another's house with one, the normal practice being to leave it in the bunkhouse or near the door of the house. In the small cowtown of Murusu, the *delegado* (sheriff) has decreed that all visitors are to hand in their arms at the police post on arrival in town and can collect them there again on departure. The small bar and general store in which I lived for some months had a notice to this effect on the wall and this, together with the other behavior surrounding sidearms, seem to reflect an almost conscious attempt to emulate the "Wild West" in certain areas of their lives.

Women's dress is simple—a none too shapely dress, which is nearly always homemade from a length of colored print cloth. Shoes are normally reserved for special occasions and women either go barefooted or wear the same kind of sandals as men. Hats are rarely worn, and never spurs nor guns, although a riding lash is carried when riding. Some women wear trousers under their dresses while riding or as protection against biting insects such as *pium* and *carapanã* (mos-

The typical cowboy of the Roraima ranges.

quitoes). Some of the younger unmarried women of the interior have taken to wearing slacks or Bermuda shorts; these are regarded as very dashing and have only been adopted by those who have spent some time in the city. Leaders in female fashions in the interior tend to be the young school mistresses who have an urban background.

Children's dress is even simpler—the youngest wear only a shirt, if that; the girls wear dresses; and the young boys wear shorts until they are about twelve years old.

Ranches

The typical habitation on the savanna is not a grand affair. Although there is considerable difference in size, quality and appointments between the poorest *morador*'s hut and the house of a rich *fazendeiro*, there are basic similarities in terms of location and layout. The location of a *fazenda* or *sitio* will be governed to some degree by water, the presence of a stream or river being essential, since wells are rare and nearly always produce undrinkable water. However, because of the wet season floods it is necessary to choose a site on an eminence above the flood level. A fair proportion of ranches stand on high banks back from the river; such positions allow them to catch the wind that blows steadily from the southeast during the dry season. The older, established ranches are usually marked by a number of large mango trees. The material used in their construction varies considerably and depends on their age and the wealth of the owner. The simplest type consists of a wood frame covered with palm leaf mats for walls, palm thatch, and a beaten earth floor. This type will have a few crude partitions in it to break the interior up into a number of rooms. The most luxurious type of house will be built from locally made bricks covered with mortar, and the inside will be divided into rooms by walls of similar construction. The roof of such a house was traditionally of locally made red tiles but these are being superseded by aluminum or asbestos sheeting. An intermediate type is made of *taipa*, mud, and wattle. However, there are no hard and fast rules about the combination of materials that may be used, so that a modern brick and mortar house may be thatched with palm because the owner prefers the cool interior that this material affords despite the disadvantage of its temporary nature. On the other hand many ranchers are willing to put up with baking heat inside their houses for the sake of the long-lasting quality of aluminum or asbestos sheeting, although it must be added that roofs of this sort are also regarded as prestigious.

The layout of the ranch follows a fairly uniform pattern; the three essential elements are the ranch house (*casa*), the bunkhouse (*barracão*), and the corral (*curral*). The relationship of these three elements to each other also shows a

Horses tethered outside the bunkhouse.

Inside the bunkhouse with hammocks and saddles hanging up.

consistent pattern; the ranch house lies well to the windward of the corrals and the bunkhouse is situated between them, normally closer to the corrals. The size and degree of elaboration of these elements depend on a number of factors, and it will be easiest to describe a number of particular examples rather than to attempt a generalized scheme.

FAZENDA MIRITI

In terms of the number of cattle grazing on its land, this is one of the largest ranches in the territory, but in fact it is only an outstation (*retiro*) of the largest ranching organization in the territory. It lies equidistant between the Rio Parime and an isolated range of bush- and tree-covered hills. In the dry season it is a quarter of a mile down to the river, where all washing takes place and from which all water used in the house has to be carried, but in the wet season the floods reach within 50 yards of the house. The ranch consists of the three basic units mentioned above; house, bunkhouse, and corrals. The layout of the whole is along a north-south axis with the ranch house at the southern end. The house consists of two parts; the front portion is the main dwelling quarters and the rear part, virtually a separate construction, is the kitchen. This is a fairly common arrangement and once again the prevailing wind tends to dictate the exact orientation, the kitchen being built so that the wind carries the smoke away from the living quarters. The house is built of *taipa* with an aluminum roof, and although it is not very old, the walls are in poor condition. The main part of the house consists of four rooms: a front room, a wide passage—about half the width of the house—running back to the kitchen, and two smaller rooms off it. The front room contains a long wooden table with benches down the side and a smaller seat at the head, a pottery water jar on a stand, with hooks in the wall from which hang a ladle for scooping out the water and a number of aluminum mugs, a sewing machine, a calendar from a religious institution, two small pictures depicting saints, a round Nestlé's chocolate box secured to the wall as a decoration, and a large old wall clock that had belonged to the manager's father and of which he is exceptionally proud. At night this room is turned into a bedroom by the simple expedient of hanging hammocks from the large hooks set in the walls—a feature of all rural houses and most urban houses in north Brazil. The passageway is also used as a bedroom at night and the other two smaller rooms, where the women and young children sleep, are more or less permanent bedrooms. These rooms are also used to store clothes and other personal possessions, but these are few. The passageway is used as a storehouse and sacks of coffee and *farinha* are stacked against the walls in it. The kitchen contains a stove made from baked mud, a table, and all the cooking and eating utensils.

About 50 yards away to the north lies the bunkhouse, which consists of a wood frame and palm thatch. Here are kept all the bits and pieces of the cowboy's trade—the horse tack, lassoes, branding irons, spare rolls of leather, and a hundred and one miscellaneous items. The bunkhouse is also the dormitory for all hands, including the grown sons of the rancher and any visiting men.

The front of the house and the bunkhouse, which face east, is fenced off by barbed wire, which prevents livestock from straying into the buildings. The area between the house and the bunkhouse is also fenced off and here the salted meat is put out on frames to dry in the sun. On the southern side of the house is another small enclosure that contains two lemon trees and some pimiento bushes.

About 75 yards to the north of the bunkhouse lie the corrals. In the corner nearest to the bunkhouse is a shed for calves. There are two corrals of about equal size, joined by a gate. Other gates give out onto the open savanna or into paddocks and larger enclosures.

Besides the cattle there are chickens, pigs, and sheep. No attempt has been made to do any serious cultivation, although this would be quite possible on the forested slopes of the hills behind the ranch. Wild deer and pig are occasionally hunted and during the dry season the Rio Parime is a good source of fish.

The *vaqueiro* or *capataz*, as the manager of a *retiro* is more correctly called, is an oldish man of basically European descent as is his wife, who claims to be of pure Portuguese lineage. One of their daughters has blond hair and blue eyes and has been nicknamed "Americana." Except for a married daughter, all the children live with their parents—two adolescent sons, two adolescent daughters, and five young boys. There is also a foster son of Amerindian parentage. There are no hired hands, for the *capataz*'s family provides an adequate work force. The *capataz* himself is paid NCr$ 270 a year. His sons get no regular wage (although they do most of the work), but are paid by the hour when employed to do tasks such as roundup, which it is assumed that the *capataz* cannot manage single-handed. The *capataz* also receives a small cash bonus for each calf born and living at the end of the year, his house, basic food (meat, *farinha*, sugar, and coffee), and saddlery (which he has to make himself). These conditions are hard —perhaps as harsh as any seen in the territory—but there are many opportunities for ameliorating them that have not been taken. For example, the *capataz* has the right to the milk of as many cows as he likes to milk (only a few are milked) and to make cheese for sale or for home consumption (none is made). A more varied diet could be achieved by keeping a vegetable garden or cultivating a forest plot, for which both time and labor are available. Nor would it require much effort to put the walls of the house back in order and stop the rain coming in. It would be wrong to lay all the blame for this lethargic lack of initiative on the *capataz*. There is some force in his argument that lays the blame for his plight on the absentee landlord and on his lack of security of tenure and some justification for his unwillingness to put himself out for the landlord while things are just bearable. However, it is clear that in many ways he is cutting off his nose to spite his face.

FAZENDA MONTE VERDE

This ranch lies in the hilly region of the territory not far from Guyana, where the frontier is marked by the Rio Maú. This region offers a sharp contrast to the flat and open savannas of the regions along the Rio Branco and the Urari-coera. Here steep-sided rocky hills, forest, and stretches of open grassland intermix with each other. The rainfall in this area is said to be higher and more evenly distributed through the year and the pasture richer. Although the cattle in the area fatten more quickly, it is possible, because of the large amount of unusable land, that the number of head of cattle per square mile is overall lower than on the *lavrado*.

The Fazenda Monte Verde stands on a flat triangular piece of land with two sides formed by mountain slopes; on the third side it drops away into a river valley. The open end of the triangle lies approximately to the southwest. The three basic ranch units are present here; to the southwest lies the ranch house, to the northeast stands the bunkhouse, and a little to the northwest of it are the corrals. However, there are quite a number of other buildings and the whole establishment is far more elaborate than Fazenda Miriti.

The ranch house is constructed from locally made brick, covered with mortar and painted white, and the roof is of aluminum sheeting. The main part of the house is rectangular with a pitched roof and consists of five rooms; three small ones on the eastern side are bedrooms, although one is used as a storeroom; the two on the western side are a living room and a dining room. At each end of the house is a lean-to, the southern one being the kitchen and the northern a veranda. The veranda contains two wooden benches, but there are also two deck chairs that are brought out from the living room as required. The living room contains a table with a radio and a heap of old magazines set on it. Some sacks of *farinha* are piled in one corner. On the walls are two calendars, an old torn map of the world, a number of framed and tinted photographs of various relations, three pictures of saints, and on a shelf two small molded figures, one of St. George and the other of an unidentified woman wearing a period costume. The dining room furnishings consist of a table and benches, another table on which stands the water pot, and a shelf above it for metal cups. There is also a china cupboard, a standard article of furniture in any of the more well-to-do ranching houses. The kitchen is well stocked with the usual culinary equipment.

The bedroom that is used as a storeroom contains a chest of drawers with a mirror on it. On the walls are shelves full of such trade goods as cloth, scent, lipstick, and combs, with which the owner, Senhor Brito, buys the *farinha* he needs from *caboclos*. On the floor stand sacks of *farinha*, as well as supplies of rice and coffee. The middle bedroom contains a bed (a relatively rare item outside Bôa Vista). The end bedroom, which is accessible only from the middle one, contains hammocks and chests of spare clothing. The windows are small and have shutters that are kept closed most of the time; this, together with the aluminum roof, means that the interior of the house is unpleasanly hot during the middle of the day. Close to the house are three other small constructions—an earth closet, a shed for pigs, and a shed that is used as a storehouse and for the preparation of leather, although a *caboclo* family once camped in it for several days of my stay. On the western side of the house are a row of orange trees and two mango trees.

The bunkhouse is a fairly elaborate affair, mainly because the first *vaqueiro* Senhor Brito employed had been married. It is made from *taipa* with a *buriti* palm roof and is a more pleasant place to spend the middle of the day than the main house. The southern end of the bunkhouse consists of a large veranda with a waist-high wall; at the other end is the kitchen. In between are two small rooms on the eastern side of the house that are currently used to store rice and beans in bulk. The third room runs the full length of the house from veranda to kitchen and is the living and sleeping quarters of the *vaqueiro* and the other hired hands. Alongside the bunkhouse is an open thatched shed, where such items as saddlery, a large pestle and mortar, and all the usual agricultural and ranching equipment are kept. One end of this shed is also used as a stable where horses can be tethered out of the sun and while they are being tacked up. To the northwest of the bunkhouse lie the corrals and beyond them a trail leads across a low divide in the surrounding hills to a flattish piece of land where an airstrip has been cut. Air is Senhor Brito's main link with the outside world, although a very bad jeep trail now reaches within a few miles of the ranch.

As is usual with the ranchers of the area, Senhor Brito has no very exact idea of the number of cattle he owns, and although he says 600 head it may be as many as 1,000. There are plenty of pigs and chickens, which, rather than being allowed to scavenge for themselves, are fed every day, the former on squash and the latter on corn. There are no goats, since Senhor Brito regards them as destructive. Water is carried from a small creek that runs down the side of the ranch area, and located near the watering place is a garden raised on stilts where are grown onions and brassicas of various sorts. Between the ranch and the river to the south are some paddocks with sown grasses, where calves, horses, and sick animals are kept. Beyond the river, in an extensive patch of forest in a bend in the river, a large field is cut each year; rice, corn, and beans are the main crops grown. No cassava is grown because it needs a lot of preparation and Senhor Brito finds it easier and cheaper to buy prepared *farinha* from the *caboclos*.

The best food I ate in the territory was at the table of Senhor Brito. There is alway a large variety of dishes on the table—chicken, pork, beef, eggs, beans, rice, curds and whey, and cheese—and at not a single meal was the diet reduced to the usual dried beef and *farinha* that is the standard diet at so many ranches. This high standard of living is entirely the result of Senhor Brito's initiative and the need to feed a large labor force, for as well as the ranch, Senhor Brito operates a diamond mine at which he employs a score of men during the dry season. The ranch provides the food for this labor force, although they do not eat as well as those living at the ranch.

Senhor Brito has no grown sons on whom he can rely for help; he has three daughters by his first wife. One is married and living outside the territory and the other two are at school in Bôa Vista during much of the year. His present common-law wife, locally known as an *amigada*, is a *cabocla* of Macusi descent and he has three young children by her. The work force at the *fazenda* consists of a *vaqueiro* and three laborers. Senhor Brito himself does a fair amount of physical work, although he regards himself as being in poor health and unable to do very much. He is a kind man and adores his young children; this paternalism extends to the treatment of the ranch hands, whom he prides himself on treating well. The *vaqueiro* is paid by the traditional method of one calf in four, a system that is locally know as *sorte* (discussed further in Chapters 7 and 10), and full board and lodging. The *vaqueiro* himself must arrange and pay for additional help that he may need; in this case he pays the other hands to do the milking. Senhor Brito pays the other laborers NCr$ 3 a day plus full board and lodging, which is a good wage by the standards of the territory.

FAZENDA BÔA ESPERANÇA

Although Fazenda Monte Verde represents a progressive ranch working within the framework of the traditional system of the territory, there are today a number of ranching enterprises that are trying to break with the old organization. An example of such a ranch is Fazenda Bôa Esperança which belongs to a commercial firm with headquarters in Manaus and a branch office in Bôa Vista. The founder of this firm is now dead and the main commercial concern, transportation, is managed by his sons, while his brother looks after the ranching interest. The firm's ranch, which lies not far from the township of Murusu, is managed by the stepson of the founder's brother. The *fazenda* is rarely visited by other members of the family and the young manager has a fairly free hand in the running of the ranch. He attended university in Manaus, has done extremely well for himself by marrying the daughter of one of the richest ranchers in the territory, and by local standards he is extremely ambitious, which probably accounts for the certain amount of ill-feeling toward him which exists in the neighborhood.

The ranch house is very new and parts of it are still not completed. It is built of adobe covered with mortar and painted white with an aluminum sheeting roof. The whole building is rather squat, with the windows small and high in the walls and the heat inside is not helped by the interior layout, which effectively blocks all through breeze. The inside is spacious but one gets the impression of a second house built inside the first. There is a wide passageway around three sides of the house and in the middle a block of bedrooms with shuttered windows looking out onto the passage. The passage space on the north side is not yet finished, that on the west is used as a dining room and that on the south as a living room. The contents of the house are considerably more luxurious than those found in most ranch houses. Although there is a pottery water jar, there is also a large kerosene-burning refrigerator, which is partly filled with bottles of drinking water, while the rest of the space is usually filled with fresh meat. There are four rocking chairs, two basketwork chairs and a basketwork sofa, and various upright chairs, including some folding metal ones. The ubiquitous china cupboard contains a better selection of ware than is normally found, and one of the number of small tables is used as a desk. There are no fewer than four radio sets, including a large cabinet one standing on the floor. There is a small library of about twenty books, including a dictionary, and also a selection of up-to-date magazines such as *Manchete*. The decorations include plastic flowers and, on the walls, a framed photograph of the firm's founder, several pictures of holy scenes, including the Last Supper, a view of Rio de Janeiro with the Corcovado in the foreground, and a very still life of some rather unreal looking fruit. There are two looking glasses on the walls and an attempt has been made to hang curtains for the windows.

At least one of the bedrooms contains a bed but the traditional hammock hooks have been built into the walls both in the passageway and in the bedrooms.

The kitchen, made from the same material as the house, is situated at the west end but separated from the living quarters by a narrow covered passageway. The kitchen is a large, clean, and sumptuous room compared with those normally found in the territory. There is a cold tap at the end of the passageway joining the kitchen and the house. The source of the running water is a well with a small petrol-engine-driven pump, which pumps the water into a storage tank erected well above ground level. A bathhouse with a shower has been erected below the water tank. The other two buildings in the vicinity of the house are an earth closet and an old shed that is used as a storehouse.

Near the well is a garden, which contains onions, tomatoes, and greens. Around the house is an orchard of orange and lemon trees, and a thick grove of banana palms lies along one side. These trees, together with the form of construction of the house, give physical reality to the distinction between family and business that is implicit in every ranch in the Territory but that rarely receives such concrete expression. At Bôa Esperança occupants of the house are visually as well as spatially cut off from the ranching activities.

To the southeast of the house and on the far side of the banana grove lies the *barracão*, which is completely invisible from the house although only about 50 yards from it. This building reflects very clearly the changes that are taking place in the territory, for although it is undoubtedly a bunkhouse and contains all the usual ranching equipment and is the sleeping quarters of two *caboclo* employees, it also houses a jeep and has a service pit in the floor. The impression it gives is as much that of a garage as of a bunkhouse.

To the south of the *barracão* are the corrals and sheds for calves and a very large herd of goats. There are also sheep, pigs, ducks, chickens, and turkeys. There is no attempt made at any form of agriculture and all food supplies, with the exception of *farinha*, which is bought locally, come from Bôa Vista. There are a number of paddocks and enclosures with sown grasses and the cattle in them are given mineral salts at frequent intervals.

The manager, his wife, and their three young children live at Bôa Esperança. A *cabocla* is employed to cook and help mind the children. There are two men employed on a monthly wage basis (NCr$ 60) who, although both married and living in their own houses to the north of the ranch, also receive full board. There are also two *caboclos* who do odd jobs. In comparison with other ranches of the same size in the territory (approximately 1,000 head of cattle), this *fazenda* appears overstaffed. In the long run this may prove to be so but at the moment it reflects the difference in the amount of attention paid to the cattle in the changing system as compared with the traditional one.

VELHA FAZENDA

The last ranch to be described is Velha Fazenda, which lies on the north bank of the Uraricoera. In terms of number of cattle (there are about 300–400 head on its land) it is not an important ranch. However, it is important as the *sede,* or center, for five outlying *retiros* and also as the point of embarkation for cattle from a wide hinterland. Velha Fazenda and its outstations are all part of a ranching company that has its headquarters in Manaus and São Paulo. The *capataz* or manager at Velha Fazenda is responsible for what goes on at the outstations and is a man of above average ability.

The ranch lies about a half mile from the river bank. The intervening space is occupied by a flat meadow which is flooded in the wet season so that a canoe is required to reach the house from the river bank, which is slightly raised above the flood level. As one approaches from the river, the house lies on the right, facing south toward the river. It is built of local brick, plastered and painted white. The roof is tiled. The front entrance is onto a veranda that runs along the west side of the house and occupies about a third of the width of the house. The veranda has a cement floor and a waist-high wall, above which it is open. It serves as a living room and the end away from the entrance contains a table at which all meals are taken. At the back of the house is the kitchen, which is a lean-to affair with a beaten mud floor and is usually rather dirty and chaotic. Off the veranda are three bedrooms that are more or less devoid of furniture except for hammocks. Clothes not being used are kept in suitcases or suspended on lines run across the room.

About 50 yards to the west of the house is the bunkhouse. This is mainly constructed of wood, although some of it is *taipa*; the roof is partly thatched and partly covered with corrugated iron sheeting. Part of the bunkhouse is used as a storehouse but the rest of it is open on all sides and filled with all the usual cowboy equipment. An oxcart is kept in one corner. Ten yards away to the west are the corrals with a shed and an enclosure for calves in the corner nearest the bunkhouse. The corrals are on a bigger scale than those of the *fazendas* already described, and this reflects the ranch's status as a *sede* and embarkation point. There are three interlinking corrals; the middle one contains a chute (*manga*) for branding and vaccinating the cattle and a swing gate for sorting the cattle as they come through the chute. There is a further complex of corrals to the east of the house and here there is a weigh-bridge, since all cattle going to market have to be weighed. On the river bank there is a further corral and this one is equipped with a chute down which the cattle may be driven into the waiting barges.

A traditional agricultural practice of the region is to plant crops in disused corrals, where the ground is highly manured. This use of old corrals is particularly typical on the *lavrado*, where there is no forest in which gardens can be cut. The soil in the corrals is often fertile enough to produce good crops for four successive years. Velha Fazenda was one of the very few ranches visited in which an old corral had been planted—with maize, in this case—although several other ranches in which this method of cultivation is still used were observed from the air.

As well as the house and the bunkhouse there are a number of other small sheds that are used for various purposes, such as curing hides, and drying and salting meat. A small area in front of the house and bunkhouse is fenced with stakes; here there are a wind pump and a bathhouse. The water from this well is too salty for drinking, and all drinking water is carried from a small creek to the west of the corrals; this stream is also used for bathing and watering the

Velha Fazenda: on the right the ranch house, left of center behind the wind pump the bunkhouse, and on the extreme left the corrals.

horses. Behind the house and bunkhouse is an orchard planted with orange, lemon, and mango trees, and in the area between the two buildings are vegetable gardens raised on platforms and some pimiento bushes. As well as cattle and horses, sheep, goats, pigs, and chickens are also kept on the ranch.

The *capataz*, Senhor Roberto, is an affable man who finds much to laugh at in life and who is not weighed down by the responsibility of the various out-stations in his charge. He is universally recognized as a very knowledgeable and experienced cowman; his advice is frequently sought and his word is rarely ig-nored. Within his own family he is very much in the mold of the Brazilian pater-familias. He and his wife have fifteen children; all except one, who is at school in Bôa Vista, live at home. There is no need for any hired hands, since the eldest sons provide an adequate labor force. The children, including the grown sons, show great respect for their father—calling him *senhor*, being careful about their conversation in his presence, and only smoking secretly, since he does not approve of it. The elder sons, those from fourteen years upwards, sleep in the bunkhouse as is the normal practice in the territory, while the other children, all the girls and the younger boys, sleep in the house, as do Roberto and his wife. A similar dis-tinction is observable at mealtimes, when Roberto sits at the head of the table and eats with his grown sons, while his younger children and wife eat standing up in the kitchen.

In these four examples, representative of the territory, the three basic units—house, bunkhouse, and corral—are all present and laid out in a very sim-ilar configuration. It will be shown later in this study that this spatial pattern reflects the pattern of social relationships typical of these ranching people. Some hint of this has been given in this chapter but it will be spelled out more clearly in later chapters, and thus will not be discussed further here. Instead one or two other points will be stressed.

Cultivation

First, there is a great deal of variation in the amount of effort put into agricultural work in the cases discussed. This, of course, is partly the result of individual motivation, but there is some evidence to suggest that even less effort is made to cultivate today than in the past. This seems to be mainly the result of vastly improved communications, which mean that ranches no longer need to be quite so self-subsistent as they used to be. This suggests that the large amount of cultivation that takes place at the most isolated ranch is not entirely the result of the owner's drive.

Labor Force

Another observable variation among the examples is the way in which the ranch is manned. In two of the examples the ranch is run by a nuclear family without any need for outside and hired help. This is an ideal that every rancher or manager would like to achieve but one that is obviously not always possible. The lack of sons and the normal process of the family cycle are two factors that may prevent attainment of this ideal. This second factor will be discussed more fully later and it will suffice to note here that even a family that is well provided with sons will gradually lose them as they grow up, marry, and leave home. A deficiency in sons can be overcome by the system of fosterage that has already been briefly alluded to.

Land Ownership

Finally, there is another problem that has been touched on in this chapter but requires more attention—the question of land ownership and rights to land. Landholding as such is in a very confused state and at present attempts are being made to bring some order into it. There are three main difficulties; firstly, no cadastral survey has ever been made of the territory so there is no factual base against which to assess rights to land; secondly, titles to land have, at various times, been granted by the governor of Grão-Pará, the State of Amazonas, and more recently by the federal government, but the majority hold their land by squatter's rights, some of them reaching back over a hundred years; the third difficulty lies in the fact that cattle are more important than land, which, as is common in frontier regions, is regarded as an unlimited resource. Some ranches are fenced, but most ranchers tend to define their land in terms of where their cattle are. In fact, the territorial behavior of the cattle—a herd (*lote*) normally stays within a fairly well-defined area that contains pasture, water, and shade— does mean that fairly clearly defined boundaries exist between properties. These boundaries usually follow some natural feature, such as a river, creek, or range of hills, that is big enough to provide an obstacle to the cattle's wanderings. This tendency to see land ownership in terms of cattle is consistent with the assessment of ranch size in terms of number of cattle. Before turning to consider aspects of the ranching community's socioeconomic organization, the next chapter will be devoted to considering the horse and the cow, the two animals that form the foundation of the whole society.

6

Horses and Cattle

Horses

Besides cattle, which will be dealt with in the second part of this chapter, the most important object in the ranching complex is the horse. It is the ranching community's most vital piece of "technological" equipment, without which it would be impossible to work the cattle and, at some periods of the year, very difficult to travel. The horse of the Rio Branco savannas is a small (7–8 *palmos*), sturdy, nondescript breed. In spite of its importance to the rancher, it spends much of its time running free in herds on the open savanna. Some of the herds of horses are in fact wild animals, but the majority are herds of cowponies out resting. The cycle of work is such that a horse will spend months roaming free and then be brought in for a period of intensely strenuous work lasting for about a month. In one week two horses were recorded as having done over forty hours of work each—under a blazing sun, over extremely rough going, rarely at a walk, and frequently at a gallop.

An average price for a horse is NCr$ 100, a good horse can cost twice as much as this. A good horse is one that has stamina, speed, maneuverability, and an attractive appearance. Mares are rarely ridden and they are regarded as being too temperamental to make good cowponies. A young horse is normally backed at between one and two years of age, normally by a young man or a *caboclo*. At the time it is first backed a horse is usually given a name, although many horses are never named. Some care is taken of horses; they are treated for worms and groomed, their tails pulled and their manes cut, and when working, they are watered and washed.

Riding in itself is not a prestigious activity—it is assumed that everyone, women and young children included, can sit astride a horse. There is, however, prestige in handling cattle well from the back of a horse and this is a skill that is absolutely essential for the cowhand. The horses never receive any specific training, but good cowponies develop great skill in the handling of cattle and know exactly what is expected of them. It is a fascinating experience to ride

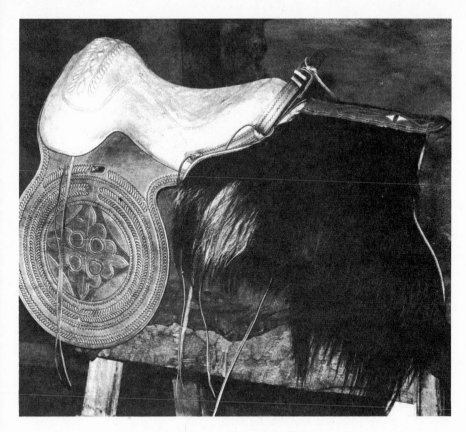

Details of a Roraima saddle.

such a pony, since if one lets it have its way one is introduced very quickly to the art of cow handling.

Although herds of horses are a common sight on the savannas, there always seems to be a shortage of horses and there is often much maneuvering in order to avoid using or lending a horse. The shortage of mounts in the midst of apparent plenty results from a number of reasons: some herds are wild and un-ridable, mares are not ridden except in desperation, some saddle horses are not suitable as cowponies because they lack speed or stamina, and other horses are too old. There is also a constant loss of horses from various natural causes, from the system of usage that means that each cowboy requires several horses, and from the fact that a number are injured in the course of their work. Some injuries inevitably result from their dangerous occupation, but far more result from care-less inattention to fitting saddles. There are few horses whose backs do not bear the scars of saddle sores; frequently such wounds are so bad that they never fully heal and even after a year at grass open up again as soon as a saddle is put on them.

The saddle that is the cause of this trouble is a local product. It has a wooden frame, covered with hide and is very light compared with the Spanish or North American cowboy saddle. The pommel and cantle are high by the standards of the normal American and European riding saddle, and the rider is held firmly in the fore-and-aft position. Even though the saddle is often harmful to the horse, it is extremely comfortable for the rider and also provides a very secure seat from which the cowboy can work. The saddle is secured on the horse by two girths, one running directly under the belly and the other further back. Stirrups are small and many cowboys ride barefoot with only their big toes in the stirrups. The seat, unlike that normally adopted by European and North American riders, is well back and the leg is at full length. The bridle is often very crude: a bit is rarely used and in place of it there is a loop that goes over the horse's nose with a strap running over the head behind the ears to hold it in place. Double reins are attached to the nose band and these meet in a metal ring, where the rider holds them. Although crude and untidy, it is an extremely strong and effective harness, easy to make and easy to mend, and with most of the essential parts duplicated. As well as the bridle, the horse also wears a head halter, to which is attached a long leather rein. This item is used mainly for leading the horse, tying it up, or holding it. When one is riding, the rein is coiled and placed around the pommel; if one is thrown off, it is vital to hang on to this rein or one might have a very long walk home.

The usual riding technique is on a very loose rein, the reins being held by one hand (usually the left) near the ring, relatively high and slightly to one side. This style is maintained at any speed, the horse being given complete freedom to choose its own path. In order to stop or change direction, the other hand gathers the reins lower down and pulls as required. For a very abrupt stop the rider uses his whole weight, pivoting the body in the saddle, the upper part of the body going back and the legs forward.

Horses are expected to carry more than just the rider. Behind some saddles there are goatskin or other hide coverings, on which are carried saddlebags and other goods. The saddle itself has numerous thongs of leather hanging from it, which are used for securing loads. In particular there are three thongs at the rear of the saddle for fixing on the saddlebag, and the lasso, when not in use, is tied on top of the saddlebag by one of these. When in use, the lasso is fixed to a metal ring just in front of the rider's right leg. Hobbles are invariably found, usually hanging from the bridle. Most horses need hobbles at night if they are not kept in an enclosure of some sort. Usually only the front legs are hobbled, but with a horse that is inclined to run away—and a determined horse can travel a long way with hobbles on and can easily outrun a man—a diagonal hobble is also fitted.

The general appearance of the horse when fully equipped is no tidier than is that of his rider but, as has been said, the equipment is functionally effective, simple, and most of it is readily repaired or replaced. The various metal rings and stirrups are the only items that are not made from local materials, wood and leather.

Cattle

Although the horse is an essential part of the whole ranching complex, it is only a tool. It is in terms of cattle that the whole system must finally be understood and through cattle that one can reach an understanding of Roraima's culture, since they influence its settlement patterns, its socioeconomic organization, its values, and its attitudes.

As mentioned in Chapter 2, the first cattle arrived in the Rio Branco basin in 1787. Many of the cattle in the territory today are probably direct descendants of this first herd. The first cattle were Spanish, a variety that is known in North America as the Texas Longhorn. In Brazil these cattle are usually known as *pé duro* or *crioulo*: they are long-legged, rangy beasts of assorted coloring and with a wide spread of horns. The growth in numbers during the first hundred years in the area indicates that they have adapted themselves extremely well to the Rio Branco environment. This adaptation is even more apparent when one realizes that the ranching technique requires the cattle to fend entirely for themselves on the open savanna. Today there are still completely wild herds that are never rounded up and that carry no brand; these are said to have been even more numerous in the past. Even those cattle that have an owner and are regularly rounded up are half wild.

A Roraima cowpony. This is an exceptionally good and well-equipped animal.

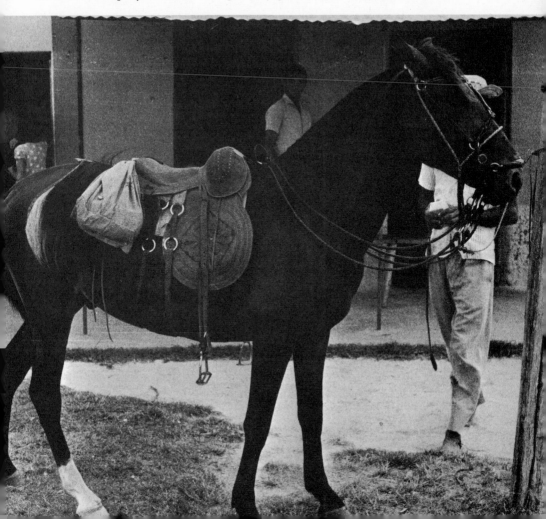

The cattle are very agile and have a turn of speed that makes a fast horse essential. Although these qualities have permitted an excellent adjustment to the Rio Branco environment, they are not ideal qualities for a cattle industry. At various times other breeds of cattle have been introduced into the region with the hope of improving the strain—Hollands, Jerseys, Herefords, and different kinds of Zebu. Although one can recognize traces of these breeds in the existing herds, the attempts all failed, basically because the new animals quickly succumbed to the dangers of the environment. The most successful attempt to improve the breed has been with the introduction of Zebu-*crioulo* crosses (usually referred to as *mestiços*), and the herds of the more progressive ranchers are slowly becoming *mestiços*. This crossbreed tends to be slower and quieter and to carry more weight, but its advantages have not been universally accepted. Many of the traditional ranchers claim that *crioulo* meat is sweeter and that the *mestiço* breeds more slowly and requires more attention. Because of the claimed organizations of the cattle herds, it is not possible to improve a herd by simply introducing a good bull into it. The cattle live in herds (*lote*) of 20 to 100 or more head, and each *lote* has its own territory. The ranchers claim that each *lote* has a leader, and that the slower and more peaceful Zebu or *mestiço* bull is chased away by the more active and fiercer *crioulo* bull. It was quite impossible in the course of the fieldwork to assess whether or not this description of herd organization has any foundation in truth, but the implication is that in order to improve the stock the system of open range ranching must disappear. The argument against this change is conducted in economic terms and it is probably true to say that few ranchers could afford to turn over from open range ranching and fence their land. The economic argument applies equally to the introduction of breeding animals, since few ranchers can afford the cost of buying a bull from outside the territory, shipping it, taking a risk on its early demise, and waiting for a long time for a return on the investment. The economic problems facing the rancher will be discussed further on.

Unlike horses, cattle are not named but, as one might expect in a society so dependent on cattle, there is an intricate scheme of classification, the principles of which are sex, age, color, and shape of horns. The basic sex distinction is between *boi* and *vaca*; the term *touro* is virtually never used and if the breeding qualities are to be emphasized the word *reprodutor* is used. The term *chamurro* is not often heard; although in the northeast of Brazil it is used to refer to an animal castrated very late in life, in Roraima it seems to refer to an old castrated animal that is used for draught purposes. Nature and function are interlinked, since castrated animals not used in this way would have been sent to market when younger. Otherwise the term *boi* is used for both whole and castrated animals.

Gender is also distinguished in most of the terms relating to age. These terms are *bezerro/bezerra* (calf), *garrote/garrota* (bullock/heifer), and *novilho/novilha*, which do not have parallel age meanings. A *novilha* is a youngish cow, but a *novilho* is a fully grown male of any age. There are a large number of different colors and it will be enough to give examples of these. There are straightforward colors like *branco* (white), *preto* (black), or *vermelho* (red); *gêsse*, which literally means gypsum, refers to a greyish white with a reddish speckle in it; *baio* is a light yellowy color not unlike ripe corn; *fubá* is a slaty grey; *brasina* is a reddish coloring with black markings; *chitado* is red and white; *librina* is black and white; and *machado* is white and yellow. An animal with distinct patches of color is referred to as *pintado*. There are also terms to refer to animals with specific types of marking; *estrella* (star) refers to an animal with a small white mark on the forehead and *coração* (heart) to one with a slightly larger white patch in the same place.

The term normally used for horns is *chifre*, or sometimes *arma*, but virtually never *côrno*, which is an insulting term meaning cuckold. The number of descriptive terms is more limited than in the case of color: *galudo* are large widespreading horns; *banana* are short, thick, flattish horns; *broca* is a crumpled horn; and *chapéu virado* are horns that curve upward and backward.

By reference to a particular *lote* and combining these various terms, it is possible for a cowboy to refer to any specific animal.

The importance of cattle to the area is reflected in this detailed system of classification. The community relies almost totally on its cattle. This is an economic dependence, since the total cash income of most ranchers comes from the sale of cattle, but it is not the money economy that is of primary importance but rather ranching as a subsistence activity. Beef is the main item on the cattleman's diet, and the cattle provide other products as well. The hide of the animal is an important item, and leather is used for a great variety of objects and uses. Leather working in the territory is purely a home industry. There is no commercial leather manufacturing, the hides of the animals slaughtered in the territory go to meet local demands, and there is virtually no export of hides because most cattle leave the area on the hoof. Leather is used to make all saddlery and harness, lassoes, riding crops, the baths in which leather is cured, sacks, hats, and hammocks; thongs of leather are used whenever a piece of string would be used in other parts of the world. Both rawhide (*couro cru*) and cured leather (*sola*) are used, the techniques of preparation and their final usage being markedly different. The hide, for both types, is fixed tautly on a frame and placed for a few days in the sun to dry. For rawhide the dry hide is then laid flat with the hairy side up and covered with wood ash. After a few hours the ashes and hair are scraped off together with a bluntish wedge of wood. The objects made from rawhide are lassoes, halters, and riding crops. The processing of tanned leather is almost entirely wet as opposed to the dry treatment of rawhide. The dry hide is soaked in water for twenty-four hours and then placed in a potassium solution for two days, after which both sides of the hide are scraped with a knife, normally in or near water. After that the hide is placed in a tannin solution, obtained from the bark of a local tree (*marimari*), where it is left for about forty days. The finished leather is used for making such items as saddles, hobbles, and bridles.

Another important item obtained from the cow is soap, which is made from rendered fat.

Dairy products are almost exclusively for home consumption and even then are of very limited quantity. Butter is not made and cheese at only a few ranches. Milk is the only regular commodity and even this is frequently in short supply and rarely appears except at breakfast or sometimes later in the day as curds and whey (*coalhada*). The shortage of milk is symptomatic of the whole attitude toward the care of cattle, which will be discussed more fully in the next

chapter. Here, however, it is necessary to restore a balance to the impression that might have been given that the savannas of Roraima are a ranching paradise in which cattle naturally multiply. Although it is true that the herds of cattle did increase very rapidly during the century or so after their first introduction to the area, there are many natural difficulties that impede the growth of a thriving ranching economy.

There is a small but constant loss of animals from attacks by jaguars and from the bites of snakes, particularly the rattler, which inhabit the savanna and crowd onto the drier areas with the cattle during the wet season. One of the reasons advanced for the habit of burning the grass is to keep the snake population down, but it seems unlikely that snakes are responsible for many deaths among the cattle and only one definite case came to my notice. However, it is neither the jaguar nor the snake that causes the most serious losses among the livestock, but rather the vampire bat. This bat transmits rabies (*raiva*) of the paralytic kind. Unlike the animal of legend, the vampire bat is small and does not suck the blood; it cuts its intended victim with very sharp incisors and laps the blood as it flows from the wound, the flow being helped by an anticoagulant contained in the bat's saliva. The rabies virus is transmitted to the victim in this way. All animals, including man, are vulnerable to attack and at times the disease, which is invariably fatal, has reached epidemic proportions with some ranchers losing as much as half their stock.

Foot-and-mouth disease (*aftosa*) is virtually endemic in the region, but its intensity varies from year to year. Healthy full-grown animals rarely die from this complaint, although they lose a lot of weight. There is, however, great loss among calves. In 1967, when foot-and-mouth disease was particularly bad around the cowtown of Murusu, it was estimated that the loss of calves had reached as high as 90 percent.

Besides these diseases the cattle are also attacked by a variety of vermin and worms, and in certain parts of the savanna they suffer severely from various vitamin deficiencies resulting from the poor quality of the pasturage. One of these alimentary complaints, *coriza*, attacks the head; another, locally known as *quebrabunda* (literally "break-back"), does not allow proper formation of the bones so that the back or rear quarters collapses under its own weight. Even when deficiency in the diet does not reach this extreme, the quality of the pasturage throughout most of the territory is such that it takes a steer five to seven years to reach a marketable weight.

The ranching community faces some serious disadvantages. Although it is quite easy, on paper, to recommend solutions to many of them, in practice the difficulties are far greater, since they are only aspects of a much bigger problem. Solutions to these problems are closely interlinked with solutions to the problems presented by the geographical and environmental factors already mentioned and by the traditional ranching system and its associated values and attitudes. These are the subjects of the next chapters.

Cutting strips of rawhide in the preparation of a lasso.

┌─────┐
│ 7 │
└─────┘

Life on the Ranch

Throughout the territory life on a ranch follows a fairly consistent pattern. A good and comprehensive picture of this life can be given by describing the daily and annual routines.

Daily Routine

Day starts while it is still dark—at about 4:30 A.M.—with the milking of the cows, a task that normally devolves on the hired hands or adolescent sons. The milch cows (*vaca da curral*) are held overnight in the corral with their calves kept separate from them. Each cow has to be lassoed in the corral and is milked where it is caught. The traditional system of milking is to allow the calf to suckle first in order to get the milk flowing. Then the calf is tied to its mother's foreleg and the cow milked into a pail. When milking is finished, the cows are let out into a *cercado* or paddock or onto the open savanna, where they spend the day. The larger calves may be let out with their mother in a paddock but not onto the open savanna, because the mother would then return to her herd. Milch cows are simply range animals with calves that are taken off the savanna when they are needed. One rancher declared that he made a practice of taking in the wilder animals as milch cows, since in this way they were tamed as a result of being roped every day. Accordingly the catching and milking of the cows is a lengthy business and not a particularly productive one. The quantity of milk obtained is low, and this is barely surprising, since the cows, on the usual system of keeping them in a corral at night, spend as much as fourteen hours a day without water.

When the sky lightens—about 5:30 A.M.—the rancher and the women will be up and about. The fire is lit and the first *cafezinho* of the day is served. *Cafezinho* is the strong black Brazilian coffee, served in small cups with a large amount of sugar. The junior members of the ranch will temporarily break off from milking and take a *cafezinho*. An early morning task for the rancher is work-ing the rawhide to make lassoes and halters. In the dry season the early morning is the only time when it is possible to work rawhide, since it is then damp and relatively supple, especially if it has been left outside all night to collect the dew. In the heat of the day the hide becomes too stiff and hard to work. The rancher will probably be busy with this until breakfast time—at 7:00 A.M. or later. By this time the cows will have been milked and any horses needed that day caught and brought in from the paddock. The boys too young to do the milking are usually in charge of such livestock as goats and sheep and will have let them out from their pens. In the ranch house, the girls will have brushed out the house and prepared the breakfast.

By the time breakfast is ready most people are sitting around waiting for it either near the door or on the veranda of the ranch house or outside the bunkhouse. Breakfast, known in the territory as *segura peito*, traditionally con-sists of dried salt beef, milk, and *farinha*, all of which are eaten mixed together. In many ranches this traditional breakfast is still eaten, if not every day, at least during roundup or when there are many visitors. In other ranches it is rarely served and instead breakfast may be curds and whey, porridge made from corn or rice, bright yellow corncake of unswallowable dryness, or perhaps sweetish cakes made from fried *mandioca*. Water is usually drunk with the meal, and another *cafezinho* is taken after it.

Meals are not lingered over and the people soon disperse to get on with their tasks. The amount of work to be done in a day and the energy put into it vary greatly with the time of year. In the wet season there is frequently very little one can do except watch the rain pour down and swat the *pium*. There are a few daily chores that have to be done: fetching water, which may be done by either men or women, perhaps watering the horses if there is no water in their paddock, and, for women, cooking and washing clothes. Regular if not daily chores that have to be done include fetching firewood, mending tack, clearing weeds around the ranch, repairing or building corrals, and performing other maintenance jobs. The more conscientious rancher or *vaqueiro* rides out to visit and inspect the cattle once a month. Although it depends on the size of the establishment, on the larger sized ranches, one animal a month is killed for food, and this takes up the best part of a day. The slaughtering of the animal is rarely quick or simple and the usual method is slitting the throat. The animal—sterile cows are regarded as the proper food for home consumption, although few ranchers worry about this ideal—is skinned carefully, since the hide is precious. The stomach and guts, together with the head, which is normally severed from the body with an ax, are left for the dogs and the *urubus* (black vultures) to squabble over. The ax is also used for butchering the other parts of the animal into four quarters, which are then carried to the ranch on poles, care being taken to carry the fore quarters in front of the hind quarters to ward off bad luck, specifically loss of cattle. Unless there is a special hut for it, the cutting up takes place in the bunkhouse. The meat is cut into thin strips of about six feet in length, which are then salted and put out to dry in the sun, or under shelter if it is raining. The liver and a certain amount of meat is eaten fresh. The amount of meat eaten fresh depends on whether or not there is a refrigerator on the ranch. The tripe and tongue are also eaten, but less frequently the kidneys, which are regarded as unpleasantly bitter. The bones are used to make a thick greasy stew.

All the other forms of livestock on the ranch—sheep, pigs, goats, chickens, and turkeys—are butchered from time to time. The meat from these is eaten fresh, since there is not enough to be worth salting. Game, mainly deer or wild pig, is eaten when it becomes available, either by a lucky encounter while out on the savanna or by purchase from a *caboclo*. Hunting trips as such are rarely undertaken. Fish tend to play a more important part in the diet, and on some ranches the young members of the family regularly spend the hour before sunset fishing.

Any work may be interrupted by the arrival of visitors. The frequency of this occurrence depends on the time of year, since people travel far less in the wet season, and on the location of the particular ranch. Those ranches that are located well away from the main waterways tend to be more isolated. In Roraima the word *central* when applied to the savanna has exactly the opposite connotation to its normal meaning. On the other hand ranches lying along the main trails or at embarkation points on the rivers have an almost endless stream of visitors. On arrival male visitors will go first to the bunkhouse and then to the main house. They will be offered a glass of water and afterward a *cafezinho*. If it is near a mealtime, they will be invited to eat, and if toward dusk, to stay the night. This is the traditional form of hospitality in the region. However, with the increase in population and the greater freedom of movement afforded by light airplanes and jeeps, it is beginning to disappear, because the cost to some ranchers has become exorbitant. In some cases guests are no longer welcome; in others they are charged for what they eat.

If the men are working near the ranch, *cafezinho* may be served one or more times between breakfast and lunch, which is taken before midday. The traditional lunch is salt beef and *farinha*, which is still the staple diet of most of the ranching people. Other dishes may include rice, beans, and very occasionally, potatoes or sweet potatoes. The salt beef may be prepared in a number of different ways, the most common of which are frying it or stewing it in a thick greasy gravy. *Cafezinho* follows lunch.

The afternoon passes much as the morning. The men may take a brief siesta while the women sit and talk and mend clothes or make new ones. At about 3:00 P.M. someone goes to bring in the milch cows, whose calves are then allowed brief access to them before they are herded back into their shed for the night so that the calves do not drink all the milk. The horses are watered again if need be, and a fishing party may set off. The goats and sheep find their own ways back to their night quarters as dusk comes down. After dusk the men go down to the river to bathe; the women go earlier in the afternoon and it is an unwritten law of the region that men do not approach the bathing place until it is nearly dark.

Supper is eaten soon after dark by kerosene lamps, the light of which attracts a horde of moths and insects. The menu is similar, if not identical, to that of lunch and is followed by the inevitable *cafezinho*. After supper most

Supper in a ranch house.

people in the interior sit and listen to the daily messages on Radio Roraima, which are broadcast at 7:00 P.M. These messages are filled with all the normal activities of human existence—births and deaths, birthday greetings, journeys started and journeys completed—and they have done much to reduce the sense of isolation on the savannas by providing a continuing picture of other people's lives in the territory and maintaining links between kin and acquaintances.

After the nightly broadcast people may talk listlessly for a while, perhaps play dominoes or cards, and then slowly drift off to their hammocks by 9:00 P.M. If there are visitors the conversation is more animated, and the women sit in the background listening to the discussions of the men and probably bring another jug of coffee.

Dust—work in the corral in the dry season.

Most people, regardless of the heat and stuffiness, sleep with the doors and shutters tightly closed. This is done in order to prevent them catching *gripe* from the cold night air. *Gripe*, which along with liver trouble is the universal complaint in Roraima, is any sort of chest, nose, or throat complaint from influenza to a mild cold. The closed rooms also provide some protection against the mosquitoes, with which some places are plagued during the wet season.

Annual Routine

The daily routine of the cowhand is a fairly monotonous one. This is not merely an observer's impression, since one cowhand described his job thus: *"O serviço do vaqueiro é o mesmo como o serviço de cozinha"*—the cowhand's work is the same as kitchen work, a comment which can only be fully appreciated by someone who has sampled the local diet. Luckily, however, this monotony does not reign for the whole year. It is broken by the sharp contrast between the dry and wet seasons, a distinction that is extremely important in the whole life of Roraima and one that acts directly on the senses. The dry season, for me, was a time of misty, cool mornings with the grass soaked in dew; a scorching midday with the hot lateritic dust almost burning inside the nostrils; and sitting outside in the evening as the temperature falls as fast as the sun into its red horizon. The wet season presents few such pleasant sensations and is truly a time of monotony, in which it feels as if the world has turned into a primeval slough smelling of urine.

The annual routine on the ranch is patterned on this variation between dry and wet seasons. The most active period of the year, and this is true of both work and play, is the dry season. The busiest time of the year is the main roundup, which takes place in the dry season, in the months of December, January, February, and March. Although this is a time of very strenuous work for long hours beneath a burning sun, it is carried out collectively; however long they have worked, the cowhands at roundup always find time for practical jokes and laughter. This is also the time of year when the *vaqueiro* will receive his pay.

A smaller roundup also takes place in the wet season in order to select cattle for market. It is necessary to do this in the wet season because, as has already been mentioned, only at this time of year is it possible to ship cattle to Manaus. A few cattle are rounded up and driven to market in Bôa Vista during the dry

Mud—work in the corral in the wet season.

A cowboy chasing a cow during roundup.

season, but as far as possible ranchers prefer to send their cattle to Manaus. There are two reasons for this: the controlled price of meat in Bôa Vista is very low, and the rancher prefers not to sell cattle during the dry season when their weight is at its lowest. The best time to ship is at the very end of the wet season, when the cattle have had as long as possible to fatten on the richer grasses that grow at this time of year. Since the initial actions in both tasks are identical, one may start with a single description of the roundup.

Roundup

The number of hands required for the day-to-day running of a ranch is entirely inadequate for the roundup, so the normal practice is for ranchers to undertake the work cooperatively, especially those with adjoining properties who can expect to recover some strayed animals. On large ranches with a number of outstations the men from all of these will move from one outstation to the next, working the cattle as they go. This does not exclude assistance from other ranchers whose cattle the roundup party will in due course work. On the day chosen all the cowhands will meet at a planned rendezvous, usually somewhere on the ranch's boundary, and proceed to drive the cattle from that area into the ranch. The rancher or *capataz* is in charge of the roundup on his own ranch or outstation, since he will know where the cattle are to be found and will have a good idea if any *lotes* or individual animals are missing. The main herd is driven along a central trail and the cowhands gather in *lotes* from either side. At the ranch the animals are herded into a waiting corral.

All this sounds far easier than it in fact is. Indeed, the term used for roundup, *campeada*, with its connotations of military campaigns, fighting, and domination, gives some idea of the attitude toward the cattle and the nature of the roundup. Many of the cattle are half wild and run as soon as they see horses and riders approaching. In areas of rocks and bushes their speed and agility make them difficult to catch, and if they can reach a patch of real forest their safety is assured, since it is impossible to drive them from such cover. Even when cattle have been rounded into the main herd, there are usually some who are recalcitrant about staying with it and who make spirited attempts to escape. If a single animal is particularly stubborn, it is lassoed and held while the main herd or part of it is driven around it, whereupon it is released. Another technique used to tame a wild animal is to throw it; this is done by galloping alongside the beast, catching hold of its tail, and twisting it so that the hind legs come out of phase with the front ones and the animal falls very heavily. This sort of treatment is normally enough to take the fight out of any animal, but there are still those whose spirit is never broken. On one occasion I saw a furious cow jump an eight-foot corral fence and crash through a closed gate and a barbed wire fence in order to escape. On another occasion a wild bull jumped from a high bank into a wide, fast-flowing river and swam to safety. Often a young steer will outmaneuver and outrun the cowhands pursuing it.

Cattle rarely seem to attack horses. The only time I witnessed a horse being injured by a steer was in a corral on the single occasion that I saw a horse used to work cattle in a corral, which is regarded as a dangerous thing to do. Considering the nature of the work and the terrain over which it is done, injuries to men and horses are very few. Cowhands fall off their horses with relative frequency, and both horse and rider often fall while galloping on the rough and rocky ground, but such incidents rarely result in more than a few bruises and hurt pride.

Work in the Corral

Work gets under way as soon as the cattle are inside the corral, unless it is late in the evening, in which case the work is left to the following morning. A common routine is to bring the cattle into the corral in the afternoon, give them the night to quiet down, work them the following morning, turn them loose before midday, and then go out in the afternoon to bring in the next lot. If a large area of country is to be covered, the timetable may be altered so that the cowhands ride out to the most distant part of the range in the late afternoon, sleep out, and bring the cattle in on the following day.

SORTING

Work in the corral is always done on foot and in the milling herd of half-wild cattle the cowhand needs to be quick of foot and of reaction and to have eyes in the back of his head. Safety lies in being able to scale the bars of the corral fence as the horns of an enraged animal sweep past. The simplest work in the corral is that of cutting out cattle for various purposes, such as selecting those to go to market. This is easiest of all when there is a chute with a two-way gate; all the animals are driven through the chute and those that are wanted are allowed to go one way and the remainder the other. However, few ranches have corrals equipped with such a device and usually the required animals have to be separated from the herd one by one and placed in an adjoining corral. A number can be driven through the gate quite easily, but the rest have to be lassoed and literally pulled through. The animal is lassoed round the horns and the rope run round a post inside the corral that the animal is required to go into. The man who has lassoed the animal shortens the rope every time there is any slack on it and the animal is encouraged forward by another cowhand, who stands behind the animal and either whips it with the end of his lasso or twists its tail. Even with this method, it often takes a long time to get a heavy and obstinate creature where it is wanted. It may be necessary for a second lasso to be passed round the horns, since one man, even with his rope twisted around a corral post, cannot hold the weight of a steer intent on escape and when the animal plunges away from the gate the lasso whips around the post, leaving a smell of hot leather and wood. Once the animal has been forced into the right corral it is necessary to throw it in order to remove the lasso from around its horns. This is done by lassoing the animal around the rear legs; the usual procedure is for two cowhands to stand just inside the corral gate and attempt this as the animal comes through. Once the animal has been lassoed around the rear legs, it falls and is then firmly held by this rope, while the cowhand goes up and removes the other lasso from around the horns. The pressure on the rear legs is then slackened and the animal kicks itself free of the second rope.

Without a sorting gate a few head of unwanted cattle usually end up among the chosen ones, and the final task is to weed these out.

All this takes much longer to do than to describe, and considerable skill and stamina are required for work in the corral. Depending on the season, the work may be carried out with the corral knee-deep in liquid mud or thick with clouds of choking dust. Although it will be discussed more fully further on, one might note here that one of the ways in which a cowboy's ability is judged is by his skill with a lasso, and the corral is the arena in which he must demonstrate this prowess.

BRANDING

During the yearly roundup, which take place in the dry season, from December through March, a number of other operations are also performed in the corral. The most important is the branding of new calves, because this operation also traditionally involves the annual payment of the *vaqueiro*. The calves are roped four at a time and numbered one to four. The *vaqueiro* sits on the corral fence with the rancher or his surrogate. They hold a small cloth bag, which contains four identical wooden disks also numbered one to four. When the calves are caught, the *vaqueiro* draws a disk from the bag and receives whichever calf corresponds to the number drawn. This system of payment and its implications for the socioeconomic organization are discussed in Chapter 10, and all that is intended here is a brief description of the actual operation. This method of payment is generally known in Brazil as *quarta* (quarter), which refers to the proportion that the *vaqueiro* receives in payment. In Roraima it is more often called *sorte*, which refers to the element of luck in the procedure. Luck does enter into it, since the four calves in any one draw are likely to be of varying quality and sex. The *vaqueiro* may consistently draw poor animals or males which are of little use to a man trying to build up his own herd. Once the draw has been made the four calves are branded—three with the brand of the rancher and one with that of the *vaqueiro*. This procedure continues until all the calves are marked.

Branding is done with a red-hot iron heated in small fires just outside the corral fence. These are minded by the younger boys, who hand the irons through to the men working in the corral as they are needed. When there are a number of different herds together in the corral, there may well be a whole collection of different branding irons lying in the fire. The brands are normally kept as simple as possible because of the cost of the more complex symbols. A number is frequently used; one of the biggest cattle owners of the territory uses "45" as his mark and one of his sons uses "54." Initials are also commonly used; "JG" is the mark of the largest cattle business in Roraima. Another firm, one with shipping interests, has an anchor. Brand marks are registered with the municipal authorities in Bôa Vista. The definitive brand, *ferra* or *marca de ferro*, is placed on the right side of the cow, on the rear quarter. The first mark is placed as high as possible and any subsequent marks placed below. If the cow changes hands so many times that there is no space left on the rear quarter, the next branding is done on the right front quarter. Every time an animal changes hands the new owner's brand is put on it; a few ranchers also use a *marca de saida*, which is a brand indicating that the animal is no longer in their ownership. This brand will appear between the brands of the former and new owners and gives authority to the latter. Such brands are normally used to prevent cattle stealing, but there is very little of this in the territory. It is suggested that a few stolen cattle are taken across the frontier into Venezuela, but otherwise egress from the territory is so restricted that there is little scope for large-scale rustling. Cattle that are stolen are almost all meant for immediate consumption.

In addition to the main brand, most cattle bear some other markings. These relate to certain purposes connected with the internal organization of a ranch. The marks, known as *carimbo*, are made with an iron on the left side and indicate such things as which outstation of a large ranch a particular animal belongs to. A *carimbo* or temporary mark may be put on a calf that is too young to be properly branded; this is done by making certain cuts in the calf's ear. The marks, also known as a *sinal*, are used to identify the animals' age, the shape of the cut being altered from year to year. A more temporary identification mark is achieved by cutting off the end of a cow's tail; this is used to indicate the animals that have been vaccinated or otherwise treated.

Horses are identified and marked in the same way as cattle, but the main brand is usually placed on the right leg rather than on the quarter.

Work in the corral—branding a cow.

The process of branding is straightforward: the animal to be branded is lassoed around the horns (or around neck if it is a calf or a horse), and then around the hind legs. The animal is thrown on its left side so that the right side is exposed for branding. The *ferrador*, or brander, then approaches with the iron direct from the fire, since it is important that it be very hot, chooses a suitable place on the hind quarter, and applies the iron. There is a small puff of smoke from the burning hair and a slight sizzle. The iron is held in place for two or three seconds. The *ferrador* retires, the lasso is removed from around the animal's horns, and it gets up, shaking the second rope free from its hind legs. Usually the animal walks off sheepishly to join the rest of the herd in the corner of the corral, but an occasional animal jumps to its feet in a rage and makes the cowboys fly for safety on the corral fence.

TREATMENT

Besides branding three other operations are regularly carried out: vaccination, drenching, and castration. The first of these is most easily performed if there is a chute, but where there is not the animal is lassoed and thrown as for brand-

Work in the corral—close-up of branding.

ing. Vaccinations are now given for rabies and foot-and-mouth disease, although most of the ranching people are skeptical about the efficacy of the latter. The vaccination needs to be done twice a year, and few ranchers can afford this, so many do not bother about it. The rabies prophylaxis is known to work and is in general use, although some of the smaller ranchers often cannot afford it.

Calves and even full-grown animals that look poorly are drenched for internal infestation. The drench, or *garapa*, consists of a mixture of water, salt and *creolina*, the last being a powerful disinfectant used for almost any purpose relating to cattle. The animal to be drenched is lassoed and thrown as already described; then its head is tilted back and held in place by the man who has hold of the lasso around the horns putting his foot on one horn and the man who gives the drench putting a foot on the other, and then pouring a half liter of the mixture down the animal's throat from an old bottle.

CASTRATION

Castration is regarded as quite a simple operation and takes only a few moments. The animal is caught and thrown, and the operation is carried out with an ordinary sheath knife. Most experienced cowhands can do this, but there are a few people who are regarded as particularly expert and style themselves *castrador*. The castration of stallions is regarded as a more critical operation and one that nervous people should not undertake because it will influence the character of the gelding. The phase of the moon ought to be taken into account, and one should castrate a bull only during a waxing moon. With a stallion the timing is more critical: it should be castrated only during the week following the new moon and never near a full moon. The reason for these limitations has to do with blood and growth and the moon's influence upon them. Basically there are two periods in the moon's cycle, waxing and waning. The former is associated with active growth and the latter, if not with death, at least with a sort of cosmic quiescence. Recovery is faster and more likely during the period of the waxing moon, which is also the phase during which planting should be done. The more critical timing for castrating a horse has to do with the idea that horses possess very large quantities of blood, which becomes increasingly turbulent during the waxing of the moon and reaches its most active point at full moon. Castration at this period leads to excessive and dangerous bleeding; a complaint that is not faced by cattle, who are regarded as having a smaller quantity of less active blood.

The genitals of young steers, known as *ovos de garrote* (literally, bull's eggs), are eaten and are regarded as quite a delicacy by some cowhands. They offer a potential source of food without resorting to killing the animal, and on one occasion I was present at a serious discussion of whether to castrate an animal because there was nothing for supper. However, it was decided finally to go fishing instead.

Work in the corral is an exhausting business and one in which it is necessary to have one's wits about one the whole time. There may be several groups of cowhands at work in the same corral and the frightened cattle mill about, charging from one end of the corral to the other with lassoes singing over their heads. Occasionally an animal becomes infuriated and temporarily brings work to a halt by charging anybody who dares set foot inside the corral. The temper of such animals normally abates quite quickly; if it does not, the animal may be lassoed and thrown heavily, which is usually enough to knock the temper out of it. If this does not work, the final resort is to tie up the animal. Cattle that have shown themselves to be consistently bad-tempered often have the tips of their horns cut off to decrease the chance of serious injury to a cowhand who is not agile enough.

Boys of less than fifteen or so are not usually allowed to work in the corrals. They occupy their time doing such tasks as heating the branding irons, mixing drenches, and running errands, of which fetching drinking water tends to be the most frequent, especially in the dusty heat of the dry season.

Once the work in the corral is finished, the gates are opened and the cattle jostle to get out. They quickly separate and each herd heads back toward its own pasture.

Freedom—the cattle turned loose from a corral.

The Cattle Drive

When the purpose of the roundup is to select cattle for market, the animals chosen are held back until the time arrives for them to be driven to the embarkation point on one of the main rivers. If there is a suitable fenced paddock with water, they will be kept in it; if not, the cattle are pastured out each day under the eyes of a few cowboys, normally the junior hands, and returned to the corral each night.

A number of embarkation points are situated at strategic places on the main rivers. The one that any particular ranch uses is controlled by its accessibility; for example, rivers that are too large for herds to cross may prevent a ranch's cattle going to an embarkation point that is relatively close at hand. Instead they will have to make a longer overland journey to another embarkation point.

The cattle drives from the ranch to the embarkation point are slower and more sedate affairs than the roundup from pasture to corral. To begin with, it is usual to have rather more men than are necessary for the roundup, because the cattle show a disinclination to being driven away from their home territory and, particularly in the early part of the drive, try to break away. It is not unusual for some head of cattle to escape on a drive, and these normally manage to return to their home pasture. The pace of the drive is slow. Cattle on roundup are normally kept at a run, on the drive they are walked, except when passing through a difficult place they are urged into a run so that the momentum will carry them through with less trouble and less chance of their turning back. The drive may well last from sunrise to sunset for several days, and the cowboys will be carrying what they need for the journey. This is not much—a hammock and a clean shirt in the saddlebag with the lasso secured atop of it. The distance from some ranches to the embarkation point is as much as a week's travel, and the journey is planned so that there is a ranch to stay at each night and thus a corral in which to place the cattle.

There are rarely any serious difficulties on these drives. The main problems are rivers that are too deep to ford, but the cattle can normally be persuaded to swim across these. Some of the cowhands go ahead and wait for the cattle on the far bank, while the rest drive the cattle, fairly fast, into the water. The cowhands cross by stripping naked, removing the saddle and all its appendages, remounting, and holding the saddle above one's head while allowing the horse to swim across. Beyond the obvious reason for keeping one's possessions and clothes dry, it is also important to keep a dry saddle since a wet one is extremely uncomfortable and gives severe sores. Crossing a much wider and faster-flowing river with a horse requires a canoe, which is paddled across with the horse on the end of the halter rope swimming alongside. No attempt would be made to take cattle across a river of this size.

On cattle drives the riders have named positions that they should, ideally, adopt around the herd. A man who rides in front of the herd, known as the *guia*, shows the cattle where to go. Those who ride on the forward flanks of the herd are the *cabeceiras*, those on the rear flanks the *costaneiras*, and those who ride behind the herd the *coice*, literally the rear guard. In practice, however, with the exception of the *guia*, it is often difficult to recognize the placings in this ideal pattern, and the cowboys position themselves as they think best. Status is slightly reflected in the positions occupied: the younger and more active men tend to mind the flanks and observation indicated that *caboclos* are more likely to be found on the dusty leeward side of the herd. The older men usually bring up the rear and the leader must be an experienced man well acquainted with the trail.

The tradition of the Brazilian northeast of singing to the cattle has disappeared and has been replaced by a sort of cooing noise that phonetically sounds much like "u-u" that the cowhands use to soothe the cattle when they are restless. Toward evening the cattle tend to become slower and slower and more difficult to keep moving, since they want to stop and graze. During the dry season the dust and the heat make it a dirty and tiring day, but the cowhands prefer it to the wet season, when the ranges are half flooded, the equatorial rains numbingly cold, and the savannas swarming with insects.

Shipment of Cattle

The loading of the cattle onto the barges at the embarkation point is done by means of a chute leading from a small corral. This chute consists of a gangplank with fenced sides that stretches from the bank to the edge of the barge, into which there is a drop of about two and a half feet. The chute and the gangway tend to be steep and slippery with mud so that many of the cattle fall while being driven down it, especially when several animals can be persuaded into the chute together. Those that fall are trampled on, or if they fall into the bottom of the barge have others jumping on top of them. There are always those animals that will not enter the chute and have to be lassoed and literally manhandled into the barge. Because all the shipping of cattle takes place in the wet season, the operation of loading the cattle usually takes place under most unpleasant conditions with the corrals knee-deep in liquid mud and manure. Although the treatment of cattle in the territory is never gentle, they are handled during the loading operation in a particularly vicious way, and it is surprising that few cattle get badly hurt. Most do seem to suffer from cuts and abrasions. The exceptional violence meted out to the cattle cannot be fully explained but may well reflect other aspects of the whole operation: the unpleasant conditions, the basic crudity of the loading technique, and a histrionic effect produced by the juxtaposition of two occupational groups—the cowboys and the boatmen—both out to impress the other.

The cattle barges are flat-bottomed affairs with roofs, which may vary in capacity from thirty to eighty head of cattle. The animals are normally allowed to stay loose in the barges and a constant jostling and goring is kept up all the way to Manaus. The barges are usually pulled by a tug, although some of them have their own engines. The usual procedure is for the cattle to be shipped from the embarkation point in the savanna region to Caracaraí below the falls, where they are transferred to a larger vessel for their journey down to Manaus. The trip from the point of embarkation to Manaus may take as long as five days, and no food or water is provided during this period. The loss of weight is estimated to be about 20 percent, although this is mainly from stomach contents and dehydration. The main loss of meat results from the bruising suffered during the loading and transit.

The crew of the cattle barges are not much better off than the cattle and conditions on board are extremely uncomfortable. There is no living accommodation and hammocks have to be slung under the roof of the barge, just above the cattle. A small kitchen is provided, but nowhere to eat and all meals are taken standing up.

The cowboys who have brought the cattle to the embarkation place often take the opportunity to visit Bôa Vista and accompany the barge as far as the town. This may be their only chance in the year to visit the town and they make the most of it.

Loading cattle onto a barge for shipment to market.

8

Life Cycle

The Roraimaense sense of time is dominated more by the yearly cycle, with particular stress on the seasonal variation between wet and dry, than by any longer period. The outlook is paralleled in the life cycle by the relative importance of birthdays and the relative insignificance of the individual's life crises, which, with the exception of marriage, have more far-reaching results for others than the individual undergoing them. The individual's birth, for example, has more immediately important social consequences for the parents than for the newborn child. Considerable prestige results from having the child. A large family is regarded as a blessing, as economically indeed it is. The lack of children virtually makes one an object of pity, and people, when they heard I had only two children, would always politely remark that I could not have been married for long.

Baptism

The baptism of the child is an opportunity for forming a new set of relationships through the institution of *compadresco* (ritual kinship) since the relationship between *compadres* tends to be more important that that between *padrinho* (godfather) and *afilhado* (godson). The nature of *compadresco* will be discussed in the next chapter.

Baptism is regarded as being a vital ritual for the young child, and whenever possible takes place soon after birth. This is easier now than in the past, when access to a priest was more difficult. The baptismal registers in the *prelazia* in Bôa Vista reveal that in the past it was not unusual for several members of the same family to be baptized together. The stress on early baptism is related to the high infant mortality rate in the region and beliefs concerning the fate of the souls of the unbaptized. The baptism ceremony itself is a very simple affair; it is not necessary for the godparents to be present, although they normally

73

are. If the parents are unable to provide godparents, it is quite usual for the priest or a saint to be named.

In spite of the high infant mortality rate—few families have not experienced the loss of a child—neither childbirth nor infant care is hedged in with ritual activities. Although, once again, this may reflect the belief in the eternal salvation of an innocent's soul, it should be noted that ritual is on a very low key in all aspects of Roraimaense life. However, as has been indicated above, most men, and less commonly women, try to commemorate their birthday (*aniversário*). This is usually done by a party, of which the following is a fairly typical example.

Birthday

The rancher Antônio, who lives a little under an hour by jeep from the township of Murusu, has his birthday on November 19. In 1967 he celebrated it with a supper and dance. Everyone from a wide neighborhood was invited and the township was almost deserted, as all but a few made their way to the ranch by bicycle, horse, and jeep. A number of people brought contributions to the party, but no other presents were given. The guests were more or less assembled by 6:00 P.M.; the men sat around talking in or near the *barracão* and the women crowded into the house. The forecourt of the ranch had been newly cleaned and swept and a temporary shelter erected, under which were laid out two long tables covered with food. The main dish, and one without which no celebration in Roraima is complete, was turtle (*tartaruga*). Another party food is *farofa*, which is *farinha* cooked with fat and pieces of pork, chicken, and egg mixed with it. The dishes also included roast chicken, a sausage made from stuffed gut, and beef dishes. The table was big enough to seat thirty-five men; more than two complete sittings were required before everyone had eaten. The women ate separately in the house. Light was provided by pressure lamps which flung a good light over the area outside the house and the *barracão*, and at its edge stood small knots of *caboclos* from a neighboring *maloca* who had come to watch.

After everyone had eaten, the tables were cleared away and dancing began to music provided by a gramophone. Those who were not dancing sat on benches or stood around outside, and dancing went on both inside and outside. There was a certain amount of disagreement about this: most of the older people who were sitting outside wanted the dancing outside, while the younger people who were dancing preferred to do it indoors. The latter group won and most of the dancing took place in the semidarkness of the living room. At 11:00 Antônio's mother and the young girls she was chaperoning left, and a little before midnight coffee and the remains of the food were put out to fortify people who were making the journey home that night. The party at this point began to die. It was not considered a particularly successful party and this was said to be the fault of the men, not enough of whom would dance. It was further said that the reason why the men would not dance was an almost complete lack of alcoholic refreshments, which are thought to be an essential accompaniment to a dance and are certainly consumed in large quantities at most.

Antônio's ranch—the scene of the birthday described in this chapter.

Growing Up

The lives of very young boys and girls are much the same; they are centered on the kitchen of the house, where the mother spends much of her time and where the child will have the companionship of other children. At about six years old or even younger, the lives of the two sexes begin to diverge. The young boy may well start tending the sheep or goats, catching the horses, and perhaps even taking them down to water and to wash them in the creek. Before he is ten he will start looking after the calves of the milch cows and in due course will be expected to start helping with the milking. The boys and youths are responsible for the fishing, fetching firewood, and perhaps carrying water for the house. At about the age of twelve the boy graduates from eating in the kitchen with the women to sitting at the table with his father and any other adult males. This privilege may be granted sporadically to begin with; at one ranch a youngish boy was allowed to eat with the men in reward for his part in an exceptionally good catch of fish.

The right to eat with the men normally precedes the transference of the boy's living quarters from the house to the bunkhouse, where he will in due course hang his hammock and sleep. This change of focus from house to bunkhouse symbolizes the individual's move from childhood to maturity.

By the time the boy, aged twelve to fourteen, moves to the bunkhouse, he will be able to ride well and may even have the duty of backing young horses. His sphere of activities and responsibilities will increase; he is now likely to be responsible for milking the cows and looking after the horses and directing his younger brothers in these tasks. When his father is away, he may be left in sole charge of the ranch. On roundup he will almost certainly accompany his father and will act as his father's groom—fetching his horse when required, watering it, and otherwise caring for it. He will also be working as a cowboy himself, although there are certain tasks, such as working steers in the corrals, that the less experienced are not expected to do and even prevented from participating in.

During the growing period, in which the young boy's horizons and activities gradually widen, his sister will be very much confined to the house and tied to her mother's apron strings, where she will learn all the various domestic duties. Although it is unusual for a stranger to be introduced to the women of the house, they do not, as has been reported from other areas of Brazil, remain constantly out of sight. They normally stand inquisitively in the background, near the kitchen door, watching and listening to everything that happens. Unmarried girls tend to be shy in the presence of strange men and women and even conventionally bashful in the presence of unmarried men with whom they are acquainted. The girls who have been to Bôa Vista for their education tend to be more forward and their city ways and clothes make them appear immodest beside their country cousins.

Education

Many children get little or no education and the level of illiteracy in the interior is high. This fact does not emerge in the statistics of the territory, because they are so strongly weighted by the population of Bôa Vista. A large number of schools are scattered through the interior, but none of them is above the level of primary school. Unless they live within reasonable reach of a school or can find somewhere for a child to lodge, the parents frequently do not bother to send their children to school. School terms, which in the interior consist of two semesters that run from early September to just before Christmas and from the end of January to the end of May, are timed so that they fall within the dry season, when a daily journey to school is more feasible. Even so the difficulty of reaching school continues to be an excuse for not sending children, particularly among the poorer ranchers who need their children's labor at home during the busiest time of year. However, for the majority of those who live in the interior, education for their children has become an important goal, and the search for schooling accounts for some of the urbanization that has taken place in Roraima. Nonetheless, the level of education remains extremely low and even those who attend primary school do not seem to pick up more than the rudiments of schooling. Those ranchers who are against education point to various rich and self-made men who are illiterate and claim that in Roraima education is not necessary for success. To some extent and under the present system this claim is not without its truth. At the moment there are few ways in which education can benefit the rancher, and education tends to be an end in itself. The little township of Murusu owes its existence to the presence of a nearby mission school, but it would appear to be the schoolbuilding rather than the education received inside it that is the important thing. However, if Roraima is to break out of its archaic economic system, education is going to be one of the ways in which it is going to do it. Indeed, it might be claimed that the low educational and professional standards in the territory have already proved a serious handicap to development. At the end of 1967 only a single application and outline for a project relating to Roraima had been placed before the economic development organization, SUDAM, that was created to help such backward regions. The detailed planning required before a project could be placed before the organization was beyond the educational, professional, and financial resources of most ranchers and groups of ranchers in the territory.

Marriage

The main event in a person's life is marriage, since it is this step which loosens the tight bonds that tie an individual to his natal family. Ideally a man should stay and work for his father until he marries, at which time he will leave home to make his own way in the world. However, there are numerous exceptions to this and many young men leave home before they are married. Beyond the factor of individual choice, wealth is probably the greatest influence on this decision. The son of a rich rancher is more likely to leave home before marriage than is the son of a poor one. The rich rancher will appoint his son manager of one of his ranch's outstations and on marriage the son is likely to continue there undisturbed. The son of a poor rancher or a hired manager tends to stay at home until marriage, as do all girls. Neolocal residence following marriage is invariable and no cases were recorded in which a married child of either sex had continued to live in the natal home while both parents were alive. This practice of neolocal residence may well reflect, in cases of the less well-to-do, the economic inability of an establishment to support two families, but it would be more generally true to regard it as an answer to the incompatibilities of being child and master in the same setting. Further, the conflict arising from the system of inheritance, which will be discussed further on, would be heightened if one child were favored by remaining at home.

The word marriage as used here is a blanket term to cover church, civil, and common-law marriages. For the present purpose the distinction between them is unimportant. The higher incidence of common-law marriage in isolated regions is more an indication of isolation than of differences in attitudes and values. In such regions a common-law marriage may be duly consecrated when a priest visits the area, but one does not hold off the union until he arrives. The increased activity of the priests and the improved communications in the territory mean that the number of common-law marriages are fewer now than in the past, but even as recently as 1952 fifty-one of the ninety-five marriages recorded in the registers of the *prelazia* in Bôa Vista involved people who had already been living together for anything from one month to twelve years. Some of these couples had already been through a civil ceremony; reasons for adding the church blessing are many, but fear of imminent death is the most usual—an interesting indication of the lingering belief in marriage as a sacrament. Because of these factors and others (like the absence of the justice of the peace from Bôa Vista for two years so that no civil ceremonies could be performed), it is extremely difficult to give any accurate figure for age at marriage and the information is not derivable from official documents. Observation, however, would seem to indicate that most men and women are living in some form of union by their early twenties.

If age at marriage is not something that can be readily discovered in the parish registers, there are other interesting bits of information to be found in them. For example, those who marry *caboclas* normally wed very young girls. Also, the church and state are in conflict over marriage and the church has no qualms about marrying those already married to different spouses by civil ceremony. A further point of interest is the relatively small number of dispensations given for marriage within the degrees of consanguinity or affinity normally prohibited by the church. However, many more dispensations occur among Indians (including *caboclos*), whose traditional customs prescribe marriage with a category of women that includes the bilateral cross-cousin. There is neither formal nor popular disapproval of remarriage by widows or widowers, but such marriages have one interesting characteristic. Figures taken from the parish registers relating to the interior for the years 1925, 1935, 1945, 1955, and 1965 show a total of twenty-seven marriages involving widows. In four of these cases the ages of the spouses are the same; in twelve cases the widows are younger than the men they marry, of whom eight are widowers; and in the other eleven cases the widows are older than the men they marry, none of whom is a widower. A similar although not so pronounced trend can be seen in the figures taken from the registers relating to Bôa Vista. Such marriages are not disapproved of even when there is considerable age difference between the widow and her new husband. People are not aware that the marriage of widows with young men is a fairly common practice, which, given the inheritance laws, has definite advantages for both sides: the young man gets an estate and the widow someone to work hers.

Courtship, because of the settlement pattern and the low intensity of social intercourse, tends to be both difficult and long, and the situation is not helped by the conventions of courtship. *Caboclas* are often the victims of the young men sowing their wild oats, but the young schoolmistresses of the interior hold an ambiguous position. Although they are *civilizadas*, their city ways, particularly their dress, are not those of the well-brought-up girl of the interior and they give an impression of immodesty. Accordingly, joking among young men, especially that relating to sexual exploits, often centers on the innocent schoolteacher.

The best opportunities for striking up a friendship with a girl occur while visiting a ranch on roundup or when attending a dance. Maintaining an acquaintanceship once it is made is often more difficult, although a young man will take advantage of every opportunity to visit his girl and will often travel many miles out of his way to pass the ranch where she lives. Once the friendship has become accepted by the girl's family and the pair have become *noivos*, the man is expected to pay regular visits, regardless of the length of the journey involved. Engagements are often long affairs because of the young man's difficulties in setting up house, in finding a job perhaps, since he will have to leave home, and in getting the money to pay for the wedding. This last, however, is not a vital aspect for, as has been mentioned, many unions are common-law ones. João was engaged to marry the youngest daughter of Edson. He had been working as *vaqueiro* for José, Edson's brother-in-law, but had given up this job and when I first met him, he was just minding the few cattle that he had earned in *sorte*. He had no immediate plans for marriage, although he had been engaged for well over a year. He said that at that moment he could not afford marriage, although he had enough money to make frequent trips by air to Bôa Vista. When he was in the neighborhood of Murusu, where his betrothed lived, he came into the township almost every evening and sat for an hour or more talking to her within sight of her mother. They both attended dances but rarely danced together, and the only show of intimacy or affection that I observed between them was when he sat with his arm around her shoulder one evening at a dance. Just at the time I was leaving Murusu, the manager of one of João's future father-in-law's out-stations retired and João was appointed to take his place. It was generally thought that this would bring the engagement to an end and that the couple would get married; João himself did not express his views on the subject.

This case is not too typical, because the girl's mother chaperones her daughter rather more strictly than most and because her family is one of the richest in the territory. More often than not marriage or the taking of a common-law wife—particularly if a *cabocla*—involves neither formality nor ceremony. The richer and larger ranching families usually celebrate their weddings with a large party in Bôa Vista, with the bride wearing white and the bridegroom a black tie.

Death

Funerals tend to be no more elaborate than other rites of passage, especially among the poor. Although it depends on time of death, the deceased will probably be buried the same day. In Bôa Vista and the other townships a small graveyard is located outside the town, but at the ranches the corpse is likely to be buried at any convenient spot in the neighborhood—either inside or outside the *quintal* fence, although in the latter case the grave will be fenced off. I attended three funerals, all of children and it will be easiest to describe one of them.

Orlando and his family live a good day's ride from the township of Murusu, where they also own a house in the main street. While the family was on their *sitio* (Orlando is a *morador*, not a *fazendeiro*), their eldest child, a five-year-old boy, developed measles. The parents took no action initially, but as the fever grew worse the parents finally decided that they had to take the boy to the hospital at the Mission of São José, near the town of Murusu. They set out, carrying the boy on the pommel of a saddle, but while crossing a river about two hours from the mission, the child died. Word was sent to Murusu and the news arrived after dark. Eduardo, the *motorista* of the town, and the *guarda* (policeman) immediately set off in Edson's jeep to collect the corpse and they arrived back two hours later, at 9:30 P.M. Work was straightway begun on the coffin, which was made by João the carpenter from old wooden boxes. Jean, one of the storekeepers, who had already retired to his hammock, was awakened to provide from his stock blue material suitable for lining the coffin. Blue is the traditional funeral color for young children, who are referred to as "little angels," although

Dia de Finados *(All Souls Day) being celebrated in the cemetery at Murusu.*

the rejoicing that is reputed to attend the death of an innocent was not apparent at this funeral, nor at either of the others I attended. When the coffin was finished, the child was laid out in it and, in spite of the late hour, a large number of people, mainly women, came to view the corpse. The body was dressed and the space around it was filled with flowers. A saucer with a candle on it had been placed between the hands. Other candles stood on the table around the coffin.

By the time the funeral took place, soon after noon on the following day, most of the inhabitants had been to pay their respects and express their condolences. For the journey to the graveyard, the coffin was placed on the back of the jeep. Just six mourners, including the parents, accompanied the cortege. At the graveyard there was a discussion about the depth of the grave that had been dug by the father, and it was agreed that five *palmos* (approximately 110 centimeters) was deep enough for a child. The lid of the coffin was lifted for a last look at the child and then secured with a blue ribbon. At the moment of lowering the coffin into the grave, there was a further pause while those present tried to decide which way the coffin should be orientated. Its direction was changed several times, since no one professed to certainty, and finally it was decided to place it with the head toward the east in accordance with the father's opinion. Everyone present scattered some earth on the coffin and the grave was quickly filled in. Flowers were scattered on top of the grave and everyone was given a candle to light. The whole funeral cost around NCr$ 15, including the candles, the material for lining the coffin, and the carpenter's charge. The carpenter said that he regarded making coffins a waste of time and that he wished to be buried with his hammock as a shroud.

Although the funeral is a relatively simple affair and is conducted without the attendance of a priest, the memory of the dead does not stop at the graveside. One of the most important religious events of the year is the Feast of All Souls on November 2, known as *Dia de Finados*, the Day of the Dead. In 1967 I passed this day in the township of Murusu and preparations had gotten under way some days before. The stores had been doing a steady trade in candles, and the *guarda*, helped by the orphan children from the mission, had spent some hours cleaning the graveyard of long grass and weeds. On the day itself there was a procession from the church in the township out to the graveyard, which started at 5 o'clock in the evening. At the head of the procession went a boy holding a cross, and behind him came the schoolchildren from the mission walking in single file, boys on the right and girls on the left. Between the lines of children walked the priest, the lay brother, and the mission's *vaqueiro*. Behind the children came the adults, also walking in two files with men to the right and women to the left, although among the stragglers at the rear of the column this division was rather blurred. In the cemetery a table had been set up beneath the Cross, which is located at its west end, and Mass was said there with the congregation facing west. Already in the cemetery awaiting the arrival of the procession were two nuns and two unmarried girls. The congregation divided itself again, with the men on the right side of the Cross and the women on the left. The service ended at dusk and the members of the congregation scattered to light candles on the graves; care was taken to see that all the graves had candles on them, even the graves of those who had no kin present. Those who wished to remember someone buried elsewhere placed candles at the foot of the Cross. A few people had made wreaths and others had brought flowers to put on graves. People gradually made their own way back to the town, leaving the candles twinkling on the savanna, and those who had come from a distance mounted and rode away into the dark. The day was not marked by any form of secular festivity and in this respect differs from most religious festivals. Indeed, the religious intensity of the *Dia de Finados* offers a sharp contrast with the unelaborate funeral ceremony and the marked lack of ritual in the individual's life cycle.

9

Family and Kinship

The basic unit of social and economic organization among the ranching people of Roraima is the nuclear family. The economic aspect of this institution was touched upon when it was noted that the ideal family is one that is large enough to provide a complete labor force for all routine ranch activities. Sons are more important in this respect than are daughters. Since married children invariably leave home, a large and well-spaced family is necessary to maintain this ideal. It has also been mentioned that it is possible to remedy a shortage of sons by means of foster children, but at least one commentator on the region has described this as little more than a disguised form of slavery. In certain cases this may not be far short of the truth, since the foster child is expected to work for his foster father without wages—because he is a son. In some cases that were observed, this meant that the foster son was little more than a servant to the rest of "his" family, not only doing all the chores, but also being discriminated against in other ways, such as being expected to eat in the kitchen. In other cases, however, the foster child was treated so well that there was no way of telling that he was fostered. Although the number of cases observed is too small to make any definite statement, in all those cases in which there was observable discrimination against the foster child he was of *caboclo* parentage; in the other cases, he was more clearly of European or African descent. This suggests that the discrimination that exists in the wider society also operates within the family.

Family Organization

In outward appearance the family organization follows the traditional Brazilian patriarchal form, in which the father is assumed to have the first and the last word. Deviations from this appearance depend on the strength of character of the head of the family. For example, Roberto, *capataz* of Velha Fazenda described in Chapter 5, keeps a very firm hand in the running of his ranch and family. He has fifteen children who range in age from about two to twenty. There is no need for him to employ any outside labor, since he and his sons, two of whom are nearly adults, can manage all the routine work between them. Considerable respect is shown by all children toward their father, from whom they ask a blessing every morning and evening. They always address their father as "senhor," rarely speak until they are spoken to, and although they smoke, do not do so in front of their father, from whom they try to keep the fact a secret. Senhor Roberto's wife is of a fairly retiring disposition and keeps well in the background when visitors are present. Even so she does have her say in making decisions relating to the family and its budget, although she and her husband do not discuss such things until after retiring in the evening.

In sharp contrast with Roberto is the *capataz* of the *retiro* Miriti, which is also described in Chapter 5. His family consists of two adolescent sons, two adolescent daughters, and five younger boys. There is also a foster son of Amerindian parentage. This man is proud of his and his wife's almost pure Portuguese blood and gives himself considerable airs on account of it. He likes to think of himself as master of his household, but in fact his wife is the dominating figure in it. He himself, unlike Roberto, does relatively little work, leaving it for his sons to do. His eldest son is on the point of taking over the running of the *retiro*, since he makes many of the decisions and on occasion does not hesitate to argue with his father in public.

The family in Roraima might be described as being both patriarchal and mother-centered. Many Brazilian observers have been puzzled by this apparently paradoxical situation, but in fact, it is simply a reflection of a distinction between the worldly and the spiritual (or the profane and sacred) and even receives expression in the layout of the ranch. The male and outside world is centered on the *barracão*, and for the male visitor most of the house is prohibited territory. The exceptions to this are the veranda and the *sala de visitar*, but the visitor is unlikely to spend much time in either, especially if the men of the house are absent. The areas of the house that are prohibited to unrelated males are the kitchen and the bedrooms, particularly the latter. I virtually never saw the inside of a bedroom; on one occasion, when I entered one in order to talk to the brother of the woman whose bedroom it was, he quickly hustled me out with an expression of horror in spite of the fact that the woman was away.

Freedom of movement in the house is not simply an indication of sex but also of relationship. Women of the house have access to every room, as do female relatives. Female visitors have a fair amount of freedom in the house, although they should wait until they are invited to enter a bedroom. The head of the household will not ordinarily go near the rooms where his grown daughters or females other than his wife are sleeping, and adult sons tend to be even more circumspect about their use of the house, usually restricting themselves to the veranda, kitchen, and dining room. Male relatives, and particularly those of the wife, behave in a similar way to the grown sons of the house. It is not possible to fit *compadres* into this scheme, since their behavior can cover the whole range of possibilities, depending on the status differentiation involved. Thus at one end of the scale is the mother's brother or brother-in-law who is a *compadre* and at the other end the Amerindian with whom the *compadresco* tie takes on a patron-client relationship and who will not have any access to the house. The stranger or unknown visitor will wait either at the bunkhouse or near the veranda door, and even when he is invited to enter, he will not get further into the house than the veranda or dining room. The laws of hospitality are such that any visitor is first offered a drink of water, then a *cafezinho*, perhaps a meal, and an invitation to sling his hammock in the bunkhouse.

A man away from his own house loses much of his status; he sleeps in the bunkhouse, while his wife, if she has accompanied him, will sleep in the house. There are two points to be made from this: first, this arrangement means that while they are away from home sexual intercourse between husband and wife becomes difficult; this restriction of sexual intercourse to the family home can perhaps be taken as indicative of its underlying spiritual nature. The second point, which will be developed further in the next chapter, is that the man's loss of status as soon as he leaves his own property is an expression of the community's egalitarian values.

Inheritance

Kin ties within the family tend to be weak among both the rich and the poor. In the case of the latter, the economic inability of a single ranch to support more than one family results in the scattering of the children at marriage, and the nature of the settlement pattern means that family contacts are weakened. Among the rich, the problem of inheritance looms its head and the expectation in the area is that it gives rise to conflict among siblings and causes dispersion of the family. Brazilian law requires that the property of a deceased man be divided in the following way: half goes to the widow (this in the area is known as her *dote*, dowry) and the other half is divided in equal shares among all his children. The widow's half, on her death, is also divided equally among his children. While it is clear that this law is designed to reduce conflict by requiring the equal division of a man's estate, in practice it leaves the division in any specific case open to dispute. This, as has just been mentioned, is not helped in Roraima by the expectation that siblings will quarrel over the division of the hereditaments. A much-quoted example in the area is that of Fazenda Teresina, whose founder and owner left about 5,000 head of cattle when he died. His children reduced this number to 500 in ten years as a result of continuous squabbling among themselves and finally sold the residue and the ranch to a successful diamond miner.

The Brazilian law of inheritance is an obstacle to the development of a thriving cattle industry in the territory, because it results in the division of the property in each generation. One of the oldest ranching families of the region has tried to get around this effect of the law by forming the family into a corporation. Each of the children of the present owner (he inherited the complete estate from his father because his only sibling, a brother, was shot in the long-standing feud between the two leading families of the region) has an equal share in the corporation, and if he wishes to leave, the company buys him out. In theory this is a good idea, but there is not enough capital in the company to buy anyone out without selling his share. A second problem is that at the moment there are thirteen individuals with equal shares in the company, and although this makes each share an economically feasible size in this generation, they will not be in the next. The device of forming a company is accordingly only a paper and temporary palliative unless there is considerable development and increase in assets from one generation to the next. The family concerned is progressive, widely traveled, and well-educated enough to realize that huge improvements must be made if the family company is to survive; unfortunately many of the developments that are necessary are beyond their capacity. This family is particularly proud of its solidarity and of the fact that its members have agreed to submerge their individual interests to corporate control, and they point to the failure of one of the other large families of the territory (that with which they had constantly feuded) to have reached a similar agreement.

The weakness of kin ties in the area is to a large extent the result of spatial distribution of the settlements and the low intensity of social intercourse. A balance to this view will be found in Chapter 11, where the township of Murusu is described in detail. In this township, which is virtually a nucleation of outlying ranches, nearly all the inhabitants are related to each other by descent or marriage. This rather atypical situation is the result of the wealth and patronage of a single man, and it is seriously discussed whether or not the settlement will disintegrate on his death.

Compadresco

The nature of the environment and economy means that kinship ties tend to be weak and of fairly low density. This gap is filled to a great extent by ritual kinship—*compadresco*. The most important form of *compadresco* is related to baptism, although those of marriage and St. John's Day also exist. Because families are large, people often have a great many *compadres*, and anyone in a position of power or wealth is likely to have a vast number. Ritual kinship, however, differs from genealogical kinship inasmuch as one operates it as one wants. At a given moment there may be an advantage in forming a ritual tie with someone, but conditions may change and the relationship lose its advantages and be allowed to become dormant. For many people it would be impossible to remember, let alone carry on any active relationship with, all their ritual kin. The choice of *compadres* is more often than not made with an eye to some potential advantage and thus operates as a system of patronage. As a priest remarked to me when we were talking about baptism, most parents like the godparents to be present at the ceremony because they are proud of them. Ritual kinship does not always involve people from different status levels and in the setting of the savanna the formation of ritual kin ties with neighboring ranchers eases a problem of communications. There is a constant problem of social intercourse in a society that frowns on and suspects any freedom of contact between men and women. Ritual kinship overcomes this problem, because the relationship between a *comadre* and *compadre* is regarded as a sacred one and sexual intercourse between them to be incest. By turning neighbors into *compadres* a man is protecting his wife from them and at the same time allowing them to visit his ranch, even in his absence. Whether or not some people take advantage of this arrangement was impossible to find out, and so important to the community was the belief in its successful operation that they would not entertain suspicions about it; nor is it a subject that is joked about.

Economic Kinship

While ritual kinship is a widespread social phenomenon not only in Latin America, but also in a similar form through much of southern Europe, there is in Roraima another form of relationship that, although it is neither genealogical, affinal, nor ritual, is in its form and content similar to certain features of genealogical and ritual kinship. Although in essence it is a form of patronage, this relationship can justifiably be referred to as economic kinship, because, for reasons that will emerge later, this is the idiom in which the Roraimaenses express it. This form of patronage has not previously been reported in the literature and deserves a brief introductory description.

Economic kinship is an aspect, perhaps even a consequence, of the economic organization of the region and could not exist without this organization, in particular the practice of payment by *sorte*. The basis of the economic kinship relationship is the socioeconomic nurturing of a man on the offspring of one's herds that are the work of one's own arm. The pseudogenealogical aspect of the relationship is emphasized by the use of the term *gerar* rather than *criar* to describe it. The second term has the connotation of "bring up" or "take care of," while the first term has more the sense of "procreate." On one occasion this was made even more explicit by a man who made an allusion, accompanied by suitable gestures, that related the hardness of his biceps to that of his penis, two aspects of an ideal of manhood. This same man, when discussing those whom he had raised in this particular sense, included his sons, affines, adopted sons, more distant kin such as nephews, and various unrelated individuals.

The wider implications of economic kinship will be discussed in the next chapter, but it may be noted here that although hard work may make a man a rich rancher, prestige comes from helping others to attain a similar status. Large herds cannot be turned into cash, so the success must be realized in a different form. Outwardly the system seems to be a further example of the noncompetitive, egalitarian nature of the Roraima ranching community; in practice, it is the basis of a hierarchical system of political patronage.

10

Roraimaense Ranching as a Socioeconomic System

Sorte

Numerous mentions have been made of the method of payment called *sorte* in Roraima. Elsewhere in Brazil the system is often known as *quarta*, which perhaps gives a better indication of the method's operation—the *vaqueiro* receives one of every four calves produced during an agreed period. *Sorte*, the various meanings of which all have a connection with luck, is just as appropriate a description, however, since luck is very much part and parcel of the system. Indeed, the concept of luck figures significantly in the attitudes of the Roraimaenses. The ranching community's view—that hard work (as they understand it, although it must be admitted that for brief periods of the year the work is strenuous) is an essential for success, but that no amount of effort can bring success unless it is accompanied by luck—provides an interesting contrast with the diamond miner's attitude. For the miner, luck is a far more capricious lady and is not necessarily related to work at all, since one could find a huge stone within the first five minutes of one's career. In this chapter, we are less concerned with the metaphysical concepts associated with *sorte* than with the socioeconomic consequences of such a system of payment.

Although the system is basically the same throughout the territory—that is to say, nowhere does the proportion vary from one in four—slight differences are observable. For example, an unmarried *vaqueiro* will get full board and lodging, but a married one may get no more than free meat and may have to provide his own house. Further, although it is customary for the division of the calves to be done annually, on some ranches it is only done every two years.

The *vaqueiro* usually runs the calves that he gets with his employer's herd. Any cash that he may want is obtained by selling off the male calves or, if he is a well-established *vaqueiro*, the steers that are ready for market. The female

87

calves are allowed to grow up and in due course will breed; their calves are automatically the property of the *vaqueiro*. It frequently happens, therefore, that two herds are pastured on the same land; in one case, three herds were found to be living on the same range—the rancher's, his *vaqueiro*'s, and that of a man whom the rancher was financing. When the *vaqueiro*'s herd has grown to a suitable size, he will set up a ranch of his own, but he will not necessarily stop being a *vaqueiro*. Instead he will hire a man to be *vaqueiro* on his own ranch, while he continues to work on someone else's. Thus he will be taking one in four of his employer's calves, and in turn he will be paying one in four of his own calves. In practice this frequently happens, and there is no reason why an even longer chain should not work, although no examples were observed.

The *vaqueiros* like this system of payment and it offers a relatively easy and assured path to attaining the goal that they nearly all possess—that of becoming a *fazendeiro*. This is not a make-believe dream and many, perhaps most, of the ranchers in the area started with nothing and have built up their herds by working *sorte*. Indeed, one of the richest ranchers in the territory arrived from northeast Brazil at the age of fifteen without a penny to his name and now, nearing seventy, probably owns more than 5,000 head of cattle. Most ranchers prefer to pay *sorte*, since it means that the wages they pay are directly harnessed to their own profits; and they claim, perhaps with good reason, that the *vaqueiro* will take better care of the calves if he knows that a quarter of them will be his. Finally, and perhaps most important of all, while *sorte* helps the *vaqueiro* to become a *fazendeiro*, the rancher has great pride in the fact that his cattle (and thus his own achievement) are in turn the source of another's success; in other words, this is the economic kinship referred to at the end of the last chapter.

The arguments against paying *sorte* are numerous and, in economic terms, irrefutable. In the first place, the pasturing of what amounts to two herds on the same range is grossly inefficient, particularly on such poor land as that of the Rio Branco savannas. Secondly, a quarter of the calves is a large proportion. And thirdly, it is claimed that once the *vaqueiro* has cattle of his own on the range, he will not pay adequate attention to his employer's animals. An increasing number of ranchers are now paying their managers or *vaqueiros* with cash. There is much more variation in payments under this arrangement than under the traditional method. One large ranching concern pays a manager NCr$ 270 a year, plus food and a bonus on the calves born during the year. On another ranch a married *vaqueiro* receives NCr$ 720 a year all found, and an unmarried one NCr$ 432. The price of a year-old calf is about NCr$ 50, so that even if the married *vaqueiro* on the latter ranch were to invest all his wages in calves, he would not have more than fourteen, while a *vaqueiro* on a similar-sized ranch could expect to receive almost double that number from *sorte*.

Except for the *vaqueiros* all other employees in the area are paid in wages. Three types are known: *diaristas*, who are employed and paid by the day, usually receive about NCr$ 2; *mensalistas* are paid a monthly salary at about the same rate as *diaristas*, but have the advantage of a more assured income; and *contratistas* are employed for a specific task at an agreed price. All rates include board and lodging—items that are regarded as more or less free in the savanna region.

The traditional system of payment by *sorte* clearly underlines certain aspects of Roraima society. Firstly, it illustrates an overt lack of economic competition and the pride in fostering others' economic standing at the expense of one's own. However, one must not confuse lack of competition with the presence of cooperation. Behavior and attitudes in Roraima are marked by lack of competition and a sense of equality and individuality, but little cooperation. The lack of cooperation is not so much the result of a fear of others getting the better of you if you lower your defenses to cooperate (although this feeling is present), but rather the fear of losing freedom of individual choice which cooperation imposes upon one. To ignore another person and to show that one is completely free of him is to assert one's individuality, and in Brazil there are many ways this can be done; perhaps the most highly developed technique is making others wait for you. All of this does not mean that cooperation does not exist among the ranching people of Roraima, for it does, and neighbors combine to carry out such activities as the annual roundup. However, the wider cooperation that would be beneficial in such spheres as the marketing of cattle and the wholesale purchase of vaccine, barbed wire, and mineral salts has never attracted much support, although a Cooperative does exist in the territory.

Secondly, as has been mentioned, *sorte* offers a readily ascendable ladder to the top of the socioeconomic hierarchy, to the status of rancher. The life of the rancher is seen as one of leisure, in which access to the necessities of life does not require much effort. This attitude can be seen in the traditional ranching technique, where cattle are left to fend for themselves on the open ranges. A corollary of this feeling is a tendency to regard cattle as wild animals. To the extent to which this attitude prevails, it makes the ranching industry of the region appear to be little more than an extension of the extractive industries of Amazonia, such as timber cutting, collecting Brazil nuts, and rubber and balata bleeding.

Thirdly, *sorte*, with its literal meaning of "luck," provides for a society that is dedicated to an egalitarian system a means of explaining away the inevitable differences in wealth and status. Luck can be used to explain both failure and success, so that it is possible to shift to an uncontrollable force the blame for the discrepancy between ideal and fact.

Finally, *sorte*, not an invention of the Rio Branco savannas and once widely used in other frontier regions of Brazil, is ideally suited to a region in which land is not a scarce commodity and in which cattle cannot readily be converted into money because of a lack of markets. The system of *sorte* quickly disappears as soon as markets become available and/or attempts are made to develop the ranching system by improving breeds, fencing pastures, and investing capital.

Status

Where the system of *sorte* operates, the social distance between *fazendeiro* and *vaqueiro* is not very great, and hierarchy as such is only discernible in the setting of the ranch. The layout of the ranch, as has already been described, reflects the relationships of its inhabitants. The house is the abode of the rancher and his family (although even grown sons maintain only a tenuous link with it) and the bunkhouse is the male domain. I think I am right in saying that I never saw a woman in a bunkhouse, even very briefly. The meeting place of house and bunkhouse is the veranda or dining room, and at one ranch it was noticeable that the hired hands never advanced beyond the veranda without first asking permission to enter. The distinction between *fazendeiro* and *vaqueiro*, which is visible in terms of their spatial movements and behaviorally in terms of who gives orders and who carries them out, virtually disappears when they are away from home and visiting another ranch. Here the rancher retains none of his status, but drops to the level of the *vaqueiro* and any other hired hands on the ranch. He will sleep in the bunkhouse and his status will become that of any male external to the ranch's particular family. This does not mean that all status disappears; certain distinctions are maintained. For example, on three different occasions when large groups of men had assembled for roundup, in addition to the distinction between the owner and his family and the visitors, certain distinctions also appeared among the visiting men themselves. In one case, a number of *caboclo* cowhands moved out of the overcrowded bunkhouse and slung their hammocks in the calves' shed. On two other occasions, the division followed the line of age (there were no *caboclos* present); the younger men moved out of the bunkhouse, and because the weather was fine, slung their hammocks to the nearby tethering posts. It is worth repeating that a man traveling with his family will be separated from them when staying on a strange ranch, since they will live in the house and he in the bunkhouse.

Another characteristic of the system that prevents the rise of any very definite status distinctions is that a man who is a *vaqueiro* in one setting may be a *fazendeiro* in another. They are not exclusive, but overlapping statuses. Furthermore, in the interior the quality of life of rich and poor, of employer and employee is very similar; dress and diet in particular tend to be the same. The differences that do exist are represented by more durable consumer goods; radio sets, refrigerators, china ornaments, and perhaps a jeep. The rich man's house may be built of more expensive and enduring materials than the poor man's, although the latter has the advantage that the traditional house is cooler. Material possessions (other than cattle) as status indicators are quite a recent innovation because of the lack of transport to and in the territory and also because of the absence of any way for the rich rancher to turn his cattle into cash. The ranching community still does not have a completely money-oriented economy, but this situation is changing fast as a result of improved communications and small-scale urbanization. These changes will be discussed more fully in the final chapter.

Rank

While the ranching community of Roraima has the strong egalitarian ideology typical of frontier situations and the mechanism of *sorte* helps maintain it, this does not mean there is no ranking system. As a complement to the egalitarianism, stress is laid on individual achievement. Thus although there are no hard and fast stratifications of the society into socioeconomic classes, there is a hierarchy of achieved statuses. One of the more interesting aspects of this hierarchy is the economic kinship referred to at the end of the last chapter. Economic kinship depends on the joint operation of egalitarian and individualistic ideals. It involves the blurring of socioeconomic distinctions, because it depends on a man of high rank raising others to a similar standing; but, since he does this through his personal prowess and ability, such an act further increases the patron's own prestige and rank. Large herds are an indication of a man's achievements and importance, but the prestige and power that they bestow do not result from the material wealth they represent, but rather from their potential for forming the economic kinship ties that are the basis of patronage. In a very direct way the links between cattle, or between herds of cattle, are used to express relationships between individuals. Thus the size of a man's following is directly related to his hard work and the number of his cattle, but it finds expression in the form of a social relationship. Edson, for example, is a rich and influential rancher now getting on in years. He has retired from active participation on his ranches and lives in the cowtown of Murusu. Almost everyone within a day's ride of the township is related to him by blood, marriage, or ritual or economic kinship. No one enters or leaves the town without first going to the old man to pass news or to see if there are messages to be taken somewhere. During the whole of my stay in Murusu, the old man barely moved more than 100 yards from his house, but his position at the center of an information network coupled with his economic strength gave him control over a wide area. This control is informal and receives barely conscious recognition; indeed, a visitor who commented on the power Edson had in the area was never fully forgiven by the old man, and the public statement of its existence threatened the cherished ideal of egalitarianism.

As has already been noted, underlying this system of patronage is the notion of manliness, which in turn demands individual achievement. Achievement is the result both of hard work and luck (*sorte*), which is outside a man's control; thus, he may work hard, but if luck is against him—so that all his animals die or he spends his money on women and drink—it is not his fault, but he will never be successful. However, there are limits to the kind and amount of effort that a man may expend. He may work as hard as he likes, as long as he does not step outside the traditional methods and techniques. Nor may his desire to succeed become too intense or too obvious. The word ambition, *ambição*, has a pejorative sense and to say that a man is ambitious is tantamount to saying that he is jealous or that he has the evil eye. The reverse of this is that a man who has many possessions may try to hide the fact in order to avoid the evil eye; this accounts for the fact that most ranchers will understate the size of their herds and that some will actually avoid counting them.

Another aspect of this assessment of manliness is related to skill in performing certain tasks. For example, the ability to use a lasso is a skill in which there is much competition among cowhands. Riding is only a secondary ability and everyone is thought capable of sitting astride a horse, although some men are recognized as having an exceptional competence with horses. The lasso is used both from the ground and from horseback, and considerable skill is required to rope a wild steer while at full gallop over rough and rocky ground. In the corrals there is frequently much good-tempered competition in lasso throwing, and the importance of the lasso can also be seen in the fact that at an early age boys start playing with small lassoes and practice lassoing each other, corral posts, chickens, and any long-suffering pet. Skill with the lasso is the most obvious of the status indicators by which all are ranked in terms of their individual prowess. Other qualities that a man is expected to show are fearlessness, agility, toughness, strength, and endurance—all of which are qualities of manliness and can be judged in the setting of the various ranching activities.

While the ranking of younger men is done in terms of physical attributes and skills, among the older and more responsible ranchers, managers, and *vaqueiros,* it is determined by knowledgeableness. This has to do with knowing one's cattle, being well enough acquainted with the herds to be able to tell at a moment's notice if any animals are missing, and even being able to describe the character, genealogy, and life history of individual animals. An expression of admiration for a man is *sabido*, one who possesses knowledge that comes from experience. On one occasion this knowledge was seen to be used in a competitive way by two men, one of whom had succeeded the other as *vaqueiro* on the ranch where the incident took place. The two men started discussing the cattle on the ranch, testing each other to see if they knew where a certain animal pastured, which was its mother, and what was the shape of its horns. Prestige gained from being *sabido* is mainly competed for among older men, who leave the younger men the more active occupations. However, skill with a lasso is not something that is lost and many of the older men can show themselves to be at least as skillful as the younger ones.

Ranching is not the only arena in which prestige may be sought, and there are as well the usual male activities, such as drinking, gambling, and whoring, in which mainly young men compete. Endurance in dancing is one such activity and to jog around the dance floor all night, especially after a day out on the range, is a sign of manliness. Some of the wilder young men's lives are much occupied with women and drink. They ride their horses in the same way as young men in other cultures drive their sports cars, traveling everywhere a little faster than most people on horseback, and reining in the horse by pulling it back onto its haunches so that they slide to a halt in a cloud of dust.

The concept of honor, *respeito* being the term normally used, is not highly developed, except in the rather watered-down meaning of respecting other people's individuality. Indeed, there seems to be an almost conscious playing down of this concept in the area and more than one Roraimaense told me that they were not like Peruvians and Colombians, always fighting over their honor. However, the notion of *respeito* does exist and there are various ways in which it comes to the surface. To show that a man has not lived up to the expected standards of hospitality, for example, is to threaten his honor. The most serious threat to a man's honor is for him to be made a cuckold, and accordingly, desirable female qualities include chasteness as well as modesty and meekness, although these do not exclude the expectation that a woman will be hard-working and resolute.

The Economics of Ranching

The ranchers of Roraima are not involved in a purely money-oriented economy and, accordingly, do not necessarily reach decisions in terms of the maximization of financial profit. Indeed, they do not have the information that would allow them to do so, since few ranchers know exactly how many cattle they own and some even go to the length of purposefully not counting them. Within the territory itself there is disagreement about such economic factors as the most profitable size for a ranch. Some people express the opinion that 600–1,000 head is the most efficient size, while others say it is three times this number. Those ranches with over 1,000 head of cattle normally consist of a *sede* and *retiros*, because the distances involved are too great to be covered from a single center. The varying assessments of the ideal size for a ranch seem to spring from differing views as to whether it is better to have a single central ranch or one with outstations. Those who prefer the smaller, single unit regard the additional expenses of the outstations as a drain on profits; those who prefer the larger, multiple units claim greater profits, because outstations can be, and often are, maintained very cheaply, so that a higher percentage return is possible.

As an example of the economics of cattle ranching we will take Fazenda Monte Verde of Senhor Brito, which has already been described in Chapter 5. This is a medium-sized ranch in one of the remoter areas of the territory. Senhor Brito has 600 or more head of cattle, of which he sells about 10 percent a year. The variation in the number of cattle sold would seem to be more in response to Senhor Brito's needs than to the actual availability of marketable steers, although the number of these does vary greatly from year to year, owing to depredations caused by disease. In other words, Senhor Brito will sell cattle that are not ready for market, and even cows, if he needs the money. The price he gets for his animals depends on their weight and a sample of his herd is weighed, as is everyone else's, at the point of embarkation. An average animal weighs somewhere in the region of 700–900 pounds on the hoof, and an average price is approximately NCr$ 150 a head. Senhor Brito normally sells about 60 head a year (which represents a maximum of 10 percent of his herd), so that his average annual income from ranching is approximately NCr$ 9,000. His *vaqueiro* is paid by *sorte*, so no cash is required for him, although he is an extra mouth to feed. Food, at least the basic items, is very cheap; about one steer or cow a month is killed for home consumption and less frequently a pig or chicken may be slaughtered. Corn is grown, as are onions and green vegetables. *Farinha* is bought from the local *caboclos*; this is very cheap, being paid for in such manufactured goods as clothing, lipstick, mirrors, and other trinkets. The other essential items are salt, sugar, and coffee. These all come from Bôa Vista and the cost of transport makes them extremely expensive, except for coffee, which is delivered to the nearest township by the Brazilian Air Force. The price is controlled and a sack (technically called a bag, weighing sixty kilograms) costs a mere NCr$ 8; there are no additional transport costs. The cost of transport on other items is extremely high—NCr$ .6 per kilo from Boa Vista by air and about NCr$ .1 per kilo by jeep or truck. Thus a sack of sugar that costs about NCr$ 30 in Boa Vista may be worth nearer NCr$ 70 by the time it reaches the ranch if it comes by air; the cost of transport can more than double the original price. Although ideally everyone should obtain his supplies during the dry season when land transport is possible, the products are not always available in Bôa Vista at that time of year, because it is the period when the Rio Branco is closed to traffic. Rice costs the same as sugar, but salt, which comes in half-bags, costs NCr$ 8 plus transport costs of NCr$ 3 by land or NCr$ 18 by air.

In Senhor Brito's case, food requirements are fairly small as far as could be estimated—he himself kept no accounts—and probably do not cost much more than NCr$ 500–600 a year, not including luxuries like *doce* (sweets), *goiabada*, and alcoholic drinks. However, this figure does not include the cost of the *farinha* bought from *caboclos* nor the wages he pays for the three laborers whom he employs at NCr$ 3 a day. However, some of these last items can be offset against his diamond-mining operations, for which he requires considerable quantities of food to feed the miners. Other essential items are kerosene, of which consumption is low, being used for lamps only two or three hours a day, and clothing for himself and his family. It is impossible to estimate just how much is spent on each of these items in a year, for Senhor Brito himself, one of the more educated ranchers, had little or no idea. If he was short of money at the end of the year, he simply sent a few extra animals to market.

The price of various ranching items must also be taken into account. Vaccination, if each animal is treated as recommended, will cost nearly NCr$ 400 for protection against foot-and-mouth disease and nearly NCr$ 300 for rabies. Salt varies in price from NCr$ 14 per half-bag for ordinary rock salt to NCr$ 28 for mineral salt. Thus to give each animal even a *pound* of salt a year would cost between NCr$ 210 and 540; the cost is too prohibitively high for them to be given the regular supply that they need. For a rancher of this size these expenses are not great, but these are merely the routine expenses. It is the capital improvements that are difficult to afford. The cost of importing bulls in order to improve strains is risky, as well as being expensive, and with the present ranching techniques is often an unsuccessful venture. Given the present ranching practices, artificial insemination is out of the question, as is any form of controlled and selective breeding. There seem to be two possible answers to improving the breed of cattle in Roraima, but both would be very expensive. One is to cull the herd drastically of all but the very best animals and replace them with imported ones. This is being done by one huge ranching combine, but it is too extreme a measure for most local ranchers. The other way is to have fenced paddocks in which breeding can be controlled, thereby diminishing the risks of buying an imported bull. However, even the cost of fencing is beyond the means of most medium-sized ranch owners. Barbed wire costs NCr$ 40 for a 200-

meter roll in Boa Vista, and transport to the ranch adds an extra NCr$ 1.2. A fence of less than five strands is virtually useless (because the cattle will either go through it or over it), which means that fencing a single acre will cost somewhere in the region of NCr$ 250 for the wire alone. One must add to this the cost of labor and the shortage of suitable wood, especially on the *lavrado*, where nearly all wood is needed for buildings and corrals. Furthermore, in this environment, barbed-wire fences do not last long and have to be renewed regularly. The high cost of fencing is best portrayed in the following set of figures: a minimum of 8 acres of natural pasturage is needed for each head of cattle, and to fence such an area, will cost not less than NCr$ 2,000, or the market price of twelve head of cattle. This clearly points to the fact that fencing is not feasible unless it is accompanied by improvement in the pasture, which can be achieved by sowing grass, and that, of course, entails further expense.

All this does not mean that fencing has not taken place; most medium-sized ranches have fenced paddocks with or without sown grasses, but only the very large concerns have been able to afford large-scale fencing. Indeed, given the fact that the basics of life are so cheap and the way of life of rich and poor so similar, it is not surprising that only the rich can muster surpluses for such projects as fencing and sowing grasses. The richer the rancher and the larger his herd the better placed he is, for the size of his annual shipment of cattle means that he can dispense with a *marchante* and that he can buy provisions and supplies in large enough quantities for it to be worth chartering a whole truck for them. Even so, the majority of the ranchers, including the richest, make little or no attempt to develop their ranches, although they usually pay lip service to such a need. They feel that the government should help in this development, in particular by provision of large loans. It is not difficult to obtain bank loans at the moment, but they are of limited use, since the interest rate on them is 12 percent (not unreasonable, given the speed of inflation in Brazil) and they are short term. The most fundamental developments required in the area are of necessity long-term projects—to get a return on such capital investments as bulls, fencing, and improved pasturage is a matter of years. As it is, the only beneficiaries of loans are merchants who buy young cattle for sale within a year.

The economic difficulties facing the territory are very closely intertwined and the arguments relating to them invariably circular. One can point to the low price of cattle and meat—the quality of the meat certainly deserves no higher price, but under the present system it is barely worth improving. For example, rectifying the loss in quality that results from the cattle being transported downriver would only make transport costs higher. The high cost of transport and the difficulty of communications within and without the territory, which limit access to markets, are already factors that militate against improvements. These problems result mainly from the geographical and environmental features of the region, which also include such impediments to development as infertile soil, poor pastures, and various diseases. Although most of these difficulties could be overcome, correction would require spending large capital sums that are just not available and that the present ranching economy could not support.

What has been left out of this circle of woe is the human factor. A brief mention of it will be made here, although a fuller discussion will be given in the final chapter. Most ranchers and cowhands are fully aware of the handicaps and obstacles to development that the territory faces and they can account for their own and the territory's backwardness in terms of them. This realization will be referred to as the self-justifying model of backwardness. Their solution to the problems calls for government help, but it seems very doubtful if the injection of large sums of money into the traditional system would do much to change it. The traditional ranching practices are part and parcel of a socioeconomic organization and a value system. Various factors are at work breaking this system down—improved communications and nucleation being two—but at the moment, it is the value system as much as the physical limitations that forms an obstacle to development.

11

A Cowtown of Roraima

So far, except for a brief description of Bôa Vista, we have been concerned with life on the ranches, which is the traditional mode of existence in Roraima. It is a life marked by a high degree of monotony and isolation—the Roraimaense's own view and not simply the jaundiced outlook of the anthropologist. However, references have been made to other settlements, and in particular to Murusu. Although it is undoubtedly a cowtown, Murusu does not owe its origins to the ranching economy, which can operate perfectly well without such settlements. Because there are so few nucleated settlements in the territory and since no others have the particular characteristics portrayed by Murusu, it can hardly be represented as typical, but as a concentration of relationships that are normally dispersed over a wide area of savanna, it does throw into relief certain features that are not so readily detectable in their scattered form. Murusu is also important as a center for change and development.

Location and History

The little township of Murusu stands on the east bank of one of the larger tributaries of the Rio Branco, which flows southward from the Serra Pacaraima. It is sited a little downstream from the point where the river issues from the mountains, in an area of interspersed forest, mountain, and savanna. The records of the earliest travelers in the region (in the eighteenth century) indicate that there has been a substantial Amerindian population in the area for over 200 years, and there are still a number of populous *malocas* in the neighborhood. A short-lived mission station was set up here at the beginning of this century, but the present township traces its history and its actual location from a resting place for the ox trains on the trail to the diamond mines in the mountains and to Santa Helena in Venezuela. This settlement appeared in approximately 1940 and grew so fast that in a few years a *delegado* was appointed and a Brazilian Air

Force flight began to call once a month. The next important development was the founding of the Mission of São José in 1949, which from its inception included a school and later added a hospital and an orphanage. There have been both a government school and a medical post in the township itself, but both are now closed, and the mission carries out both these duties, although some of the larger nearby *malocas* have schools of their own. In 1954 the ranchers built their own chapel in the community and dedicated it to Nossa Senhora do Perpetuo Socorro. However, a more vital event for the well-being of the town occurred in 1957, when the leading rancher of the area and one of the richest in the whole territory built himself a house in Murusu in order, for his children's sake, to be near the mission school. His presence and influence have done much to stabilize the community, a fact which is recognized by some of the inhabitants who go so far as to suggest that the township will disappear on his death.

Over the years a number of small shops have opened, which have increased the importance of the township in the area. At the moment its old function as a staging post on the route north has waned, because much of the traffic goes by air, but if the projected Manaus-Bôa Vista-Santa Helena road runs close by, as presently planned, this function could be renewed. The township lies about 100 miles from Bôa Vista and flying time in a light aircraft is just over an hour; most people travel this way or by the fortnightly FAB flight. Flights by FAB are free of charge but less reliable as far as time is concerned, since they more often than not fail to arrive on the scheduled day. It is barely possible to give a standard time for the land journey by jeep or truck between Murusu and Bôa Vista; six hours is good going, but if the weather is bad the trip may take a week, and it is possible to be trapped between two creeks that have risen sharply as a result of violent storms. I twice set out for Murusu by land and both times failed to make it because the road was impassable, and that was in November, well into the dry season. By horse the journey to Bôa Vista can be done in three days, but they are three days with ten or more hours in the saddle.

Murusu Today

Today the town of Murusu consists of forty-two buildings; all except one, the church, are used as dwelling houses, although not all of them are occupied. The main part of the town is a wide street running approximately north-south, parallel to the river, with houses on either side of it. Toward the northern end the houses on the eastern side of the street stop at the airstrip; on the western side they curve around to the west, following the line of the river and the airstrip, which runs in a northwest-southeast direction. At the southern end the last house on the eastern side is the church; on the western side the houses continue, but in a more dispersed fashion. As well as this main street, there is a collection of houses at the southeast corner that forms three more small streets. Further to the east are the abandoned house of a protestant missionary, the house of a *cabocla*, and a little beyond that, the cemetery, which is just under five minutes' walk from the town. To the north of the township but nearly adjoining it is a

The main street of Vila Murusu, looking from the northeast corner.

small *maloca*, and to the south, a little over five minutes' walk, is the mission of São José.

All the types of house construction common to the area can be observed in Murusu; there are wood-framed and planked houses, *taipa* houses with or without mortar, brick houses, thatched roofs, aluminum sheeting roofs, tile roofs, mud floors, concrete floors, and wood floors, in every possible combination. The houses in the main street are on the whole of more expensive construction than those in the side streets; they are made of more durable materials, are painted, and are larger and newer. The main street and the houses in it are lit by electricity, which is provided by a generator that runs every evening from dusk until 9 o'clock.

The layout and contents of the houses are not very different from those described for the ranch houses on the savanna. The front of the house, looking onto the street, is the living room and the one into which visitors are invited. The kitchen and bedrooms are to the rear of the house, and so is the dining room, if there is one in addition to the front room. The majority of houses have a small fenced area at the back where a few vegetables and fruit trees, mainly limes, grow. Nearly every house has an earth closet constructed in the garden, but all bathing and washing of clothes are carried out in the river.

Diet does differ slightly from that on the savanna. *Segura peito* of beef, milk, and *farinha* is replaced by a meal that is more recognizably breakfast, consisting of mandioca cakes and large cups of milky coffee. The variety of food tends to be greater in the town than on the savanna.

The population of Murusu varies from time to time, but there are just under 100 permanent inhabitants, by which is meant people who live in the township more of the time than elsewhere. The majority of the inhabitants own ranches in the neighborhood, but for a variety of reasons prefer to live in Murusu; there are also many houses in the town owned by people who live on neighboring ranches and only occasionally spend any time in their town houses. Thus there are normally a number of houses empty at any one time. The usual reason for people to live in Murusu rather than on their ranch is accessibility to the mission school, and the population rises noticeably during school term. The permanent inhabitants are mainly made up of those who are too old to work their own ranches and those who have occupations and interests that are not connected, or only indirectly connected, with ranching. The latter are mainly government employees or shopkeepers, although these occupations are far from being exclusive; one individual, besides being a shopkeeper and a government employee, has ranching interests as well. Some idea of the composition of the town and the nature of life in it can be gained by considering some of its inhabitants. However, before doing so, it is important to note that, with the exception of some of the government employees, everybody is related to everybody else by ties of blood, marriage, or ritual or economic kinship, and in many cases by several of these relationships.

Network of Relationships

The most influential man in Murusu and its environs is Edson, who has been mentioned on several earlier occasions. He is an extremely rich man, who owns five ranches in the district as well as his house in Murusu, where he now lives permanently. He has a bad heart and his activities are now very limited; during my time at Murusu I never saw him more than 100 yards from his house. His great wealth has allowed him to acquire most of the material possessions that are to be found in the region, including such items as a jeep and a refrigerator; and he is able to pander to his health by bringing from Bôa Vista food that he regards as good for him, in particular packets of chicken noodle soup. He originally moved to Murusu so that his younger children could go to the mission school. Because of his enforced inactivity, he has found the township an ideal place from which to maintain his control over the area—an authority that rests on his status as the richest and most powerful man in the district, but which is also maintained by his being at the center of the flow of information. Almost all relationships in and around Murusu lead back in some way to Edson, and he is so much the linchpin of the area's socioeconomic organization that some people feel the township may well disintegrate on his death. Because of the educational and commercial importance that the township now has this seems unlikely, but that such an idea exists is an interesting indication of the importance with which social relationships are regarded. It is also indicative of the expectation that Edson's children will fall out over the inheritance.

Edson has had one wife, Dona Maria, by whom he has had eight children—five sons and three daughters. Two of his children live in São Paulo; one is a daughter, who is married to a successful diamond miner, and the other his youngest son, who is at school there. All the other children live locally and are concerned to some degree with the ranching industry. The four grown sons range in age from twenty-six to thirty-five. The eldest of these, Vicente, is in poor health and claims to be too ill for the hard life of ranching, although as a young man he worked as his father's *vaqueiro* and collected enough cattle to form his own ranch. He rarely visits the place and instead employs a cousin (his father's sister's son) to manage the ranch. The cousin is married and his wife and children live in Murusu; he divides his time between the ranch and the township. Vicente himself is separated from his wife and has no children. Because he can no longer work on a ranch, his father has set him up in a shop, but his is the least commercial of the five shops in Murusu (for reasons that will be explained later) and the shop is frequently closed because he is away driving his father's jeep on some errand or other. Vicente also has his own house and it is one of the newest and smartest buildings in Murusu.

The second son, Antônio, whose birthday party was described in Chapter 8, used to work as his father's *vaqueiro* but has given this up and now simply ranches on his own account. He owns two small ranches and spends most of his time at one or the other of these. He also owns a house in Murusu, which is situated next to that of his mother-in-law, Teresa. Antônio's wife Raimunda is a sister of the wife of the cousin who looks after his brother Vicente's ranch. Another of his wife's sisters is married to Lazaro, the most successful shopkeeper in Murusu. Antônio's mother-in-law is separated from her husband and lives with her unmarried children, the eldest of whom teaches at the mission school. Teresa's sister Helena is married to another resident of the town who, in turn, has a brother living there.

Edson's third son, Pedro, is the present *capataz* of one of his father's ranches, which lies about an hour and an half's ride downstream from the town. Pedro is paid by *sorte* and has started a ranch of his own, which is a further hour's ride to the south. He employs a Wapishana Indian as his *vaqueiro* and pays him *sorte*. Pedro is married to Francisca, whose parents live in Murusu; her mother is a Wapishana and her father Francisco owns a *sitio* at some distance from the town, but is also a *comboiero*, a man who transports goods by ox train. Pedro is on particularly good terms with his wife's unmarried brother Conrado and they spend much time together fishing, drinking, and whoring. Pedro owns a house in town and he himself visits Murusu frequently in search of excitement. His family, however, spends nearly all the time on the ranch.

The fourth and youngest son still in the region is Paulo; he is *vaqueiro* of his father's main ranch and is still building a herd large enough for it to be worth ranching on his own account. He is unmarried, is of a serious turn of mind, and rarely comes into Murusu.

Edson's eldest daughter, Sonia, is married to Claudio, who manages a ranch belonging to his family business that lies on the right bank of the river about ten minutes' ride downstream. The ranch is one of the more progressive in the territory, and Claudio is viewed with some suspicion because of the innovations he is making. The ranch house is one of the most modern I visited, but not one of the most comfortable. There is a fair amount of cooperation between Claudio and his father-in-law and his brothers-in-law, but there is also some lingering conflict connected with the ill-feeling that arose between the families when Edson took control of the area from Claudio's family, which had previously been the most powerful.

Edson's youngest daughter is engaged to be married to a young man called João, and this case has already been described in Chapter 8.

So far this has only taken into account relationships that can be traced to Edson through his sons' marriages, but there are also his own affines. The most important of these are his wife's brothers, José and Luciano. Both brothers have at one time and another worked *sorte* for Edson, but José, the younger, has been more successful. He owns a large ranch, has a house in Murusu and another in Bôa Vista, runs a jeep, and is very highly respected in the district. He spends most of his time on his ranch, unlike his elder brother who lives nearly the whole time in Murusu. The sister of these two men also lives in Murusu. At the moment she has no husband, although she has had a number in the past. Her daughter Bela is married to Flavio, who, in turn, is related by marriage to Francisco, whose eldest son is married to Flavio's first cousin (his mother's brother's daughter). Flavio has a few cattle that he runs with those of his wife's mother's brother Luciano, but otherwise he works for wages, for anyone who wants to employ him. He lives in Murusu, but is away working much of the time.

Enough has been said to indicate the ramifications of Edson's kinship ties within the sphere of Murusu, but these relationships also spread out onto the savannas and incorporate people who cannot be regarded as inhabitants of Murusu, but who do pay infrequent visits to the township. As well as the nephew who manages his son Vicente's ranch, Edson has another nephew and a niece, children of the same brother, living in the neighborhood. The man has his own ranch and the woman is married to an influential rancher of one of the oldest families of the territory. Then there are those like Temir, who owns a *sitio* to the north of the town and who claims to be Edson's second cousin, although Edson himself thinks that the relationship is rather more remote. We have also left out of this list Edson's *filho de criação*, Walter, a man of obvious African parentage who has done extremely well by his adoption. He has a ranch of his own and continues to work *sorte* for his foster father. Nor does this list include the dense network of ritual and economic kinship ties, which in most cases duplicate and often triplicate the consanguineous and affinal links. These last relationships diffuse well beyond the boundaries of Edson's kin and affines, particularly ritual kinship, by whose network virtually everyone in the neighborhood is joined. The density of this network is so great that it is more rewarding to examine those individuals who are not included within it. These include a number of *caboclos* and three *civilizados*: the *delegado*, who spends most of his time in Bôa Vista, and all his time in Murusu playing dominoes; the *guarda* or policeman, whose family lives in Bôa Vista, and whom I would expect to become enmeshed in the network if he stays much longer; and the *telegrafista*, who is a young man and who does a six month tour only. These three men are all government employees, but it is less this fact than the temporary nature of their relationship with the town that accounts for their marginal status. This assumption can be supported by the case of the fourth government employee, the *motorista*, whose duties are mainly concerned with manning the small electric light generator. His duties, like those of the other government employees, are far from onerous. The *telegrafista* does only about two hours of work a day on average, the *guarda* has nothing specific to do (he arrested two men during my stay), and the *delegado* is rarely there. This would leave a lot of time for any other occupation they might wish to undertake, but, with the exception of the *motorista*, their involvement in the community is as marginal as their position in the relationship network. Eduardo, the *motorista*, on the other hand, has a thriving little shop and his aim is to become a rancher. He already owns a number of cattle and is looking for a ranch to buy. He is perhaps the most energetic and go-ahead man in the area—qualities that Edson has recognized. Edson has provided the money for Eduardo to open his shop and allows him to run his cattle on one of his ranches. He also seems to trust Eduardo more than his own sons and gives him the responsible jobs to do at roundup, such as keeping the record of the calves and reporting it to him. Thus Eduardo has been drawn into Edson's economic genealogy, but he has also entered into ritual kinship with a number of local people, including Edson's second son and brother-in-law, both of whom are influential people in the locality.

Shopkeepers

The mention of Eduardo as a shopkeeper draws attention to another distinguishable group of people in the Murusu setting. Unlike the government employees, they are very much part of the Murusu scene, for even if they are not directly involved in ranching they are indirectly concerned with it. There are five shops in Murusu, a number that on first sight seems excessive for the size of population not only of the township, but also of the environs. In normal commercial terms this would be a reasonable assumption; but normal commercial considerations do not apply, because the shopkeeping practices have to follow the ranching practices. The most important factor here is that most people only get paid once a year—ranchers when they sell their cattle and *vaqueiros* when the draw is made at roundup. This means that a shopkeeper must extend long-term credit to his customers, which he in turn is unable to obtain from the wholesaler in Bôa Vista. Since the capital of these shopkeepers is very low, there is a limit to the amount of credit they can carry, and no single shopkeeper has the funds necessary to carry the credit for the whole district. Indeed it is arguable that one shop alone could not survive, and that even if it did, it could not do more business than it does when faced with competition. It is interesting that competition between the shops in Murusu is not carried on in terms of prices, but rather in the extension of credit. This is a risky business and requires a delicate balance between losing customers, avoiding bad debts, and having supplies cut off by the wholesalers as a result of nonpayment.

The five shops carry a very similar range of goods. The widest variety is to be found in Eduardo's shop and includes such items as cooking pots, cardboard suitcases, a variety of items of clothing, hats, rolls of cloth, tins of sweets (often sold one by one), various patent medicines (mainly of the aspirin and Alka-Seltzer sort), toilet powder, soap, toothpaste, toothbrushes, cheap scent, hair oil, combs, cotton, needles, sewing machine oil, razor blades, matches, cigarettes, rolls of locally grown tobacco, small looking glasses, various tinned foods such as sardines and drinking chocolate, cooking oil, dried milk, such tools as knives, axes, hoes, and rakes, lengths of rope, hammocks, fishing lines and hooks, kerosene, rice, *farinha*, rat poison, patent fly killers, envelopes, shot and powder, and a range of alcoholic drinks, including vodka and three types of sweet vermouth, but mainly *cachaça* or *alcool*, a stronger proof sugar-cane spirit usually taken diluted with water. A large refrigerator behind the counter contains bottles of cold water for whoever wants it, and less frequently beer. Because of transport costs, beer is very expensive; a half-liter bottle of Brazilian beer costs nearly a dollar. More often the beer available is canned and of Venezuelan manufacture and has found its way down over the frontier from Santa Helena.

In spite of the similarity in the goods stocked and the prices asked for them, each shop has its own character. Lazaro tends to specialize in cloth and clothing and has a wider range of materials than any of the other shops. His drink business is small, since the shop lies to the south and out of the main part of the town. This may have some effect on business but it cannot make much difference, for the shop has the largest turnover and it is the most profitable in Murusu. This can be accounted for in a number of ways, including Lazaro's own business acumen. He is the only shopkeeper who is always willing to take cattle in payment for a debt, and he does so at far below the market price at which he then sells them. He has bought himself a jeep, so that the cost of transporting goods is much lower for him, although his prices remain the same as in the other stores. Finally, Lazaro has managed to make rather better arrangements with the wholesalers in Bôa Vista, to some of whom he is related, than have the others.

Vicente, Edson's eldest son, sells no form of alcoholic refreshment and, although he stocks certain small novelties not found in the other shops, the business can barely be a paying proposition. The shop is often closed and Vicente himself does not seem to be interested in it and is clearly not commercially minded. It might be noted that although he is more directly related to more of his potential customers than are any of his competitors, such relationships do not appear to influence the choice of where to shop.

The other two shops give the appearance of being much busier than the three discussed so far, but this is mainly because their drink trade has turned them into the main centers of social intercourse. Nearly all the shopping is done by men, who even choose the material for their wives' dresses. The smallest and oldest of these shops is Zecão's; so small and limited is his stock that his shop is little more than a bar selling mainly *cachaça*. Many of his customers are *caboclos* and the dances that are held there are not attended by white women. A fairly large proportion of Zecão's dealings are cash transactions.

Eduardo's stock has already been described and his shop is the next most profitable after Lazaro's. He is a clever and hard-working man, and has rapidly become one of the most respected people in the township. His shop is the center for most of the serious discussions about local problems. He will take cattle to cover debts but prefers not to; accordingly, because his turnover is high he carries a heavy credit load, about NCr$ 9,000 to 10,000. A rather similar amount of credit has been given by the fifth shopkeeper, Jean. He is a Frenchman, reputedly an ex-Devil's Island convict and a diamond miner who was forced to retire as a result of an accident. The turnover of his shop is about the same as that of Eduardo's but on a smaller and less varied stock. This is achieved by a liberal granting of credit and he carries a number of bad debts. He will not normally take cattle in payment, but while I was there he accepted a few head from a Wapishana who owed him nearly NCr$ 1,000. Jean's shop is the scene of much drinking and ribald male conversation. When payment can be secured, profits tend to be high. Jean estimated that he made a 40–50 percent profit on the average, but the amount varies from item to item and from individual to individual. Thus a good quality hammock that had cost NCr$ 35 was selling for NCr$ 45, but a cheaper hammock that had cost NCr$ 14 was going for NCr$ 17. The greatest profits are on such items as sweets, soap, scent, hair oil, and *cachaça*, the last being bought at NCr$ 1.2 a bottle and sold for NCr$ 3.

Life in Murusu

A few people, such as Zecão and Flavio, are up well before dawn, but the majority of the inhabitants are slightly later risers and it is six o'clock before the town is astir. Jean takes his towel and goes off to bathe in the river, and Edson is already sitting and watching in front of his house, where he is brought a *cafezinho* by the daughter of his *filho de criação*, Walter. Elias arrives at Jean's shop, helps himself to a shot of *cachaça*, and complains of his *gripe*; soon after Aldolfo does the same, but without offering an excuse. During this time the younger girls are sweeping out the houses and around 7 o'clock most people sit down to breakfast. Eduardo's eldest son arrives back from the mission on his bicycle, where he has been to collect the milk. Before breakfast is over the children from the outlying ranches are riding through on their way to school, and the town children finish their meal, seize their books, and follow them. Those who have any work to do get on with it. Flavio is repairing a wall for Lazaro, slapping the wet mud with a throwing action onto the framework of staithes. Aldolfo, who ekes out his money by cutting and selling firewood, creaks off toward the savanna with his oxcart. This is a great comedown for a once rich rancher, but his wealth has been dissipated on women and drink. Those who have nothing to do sit and talk, forming and reforming themselves into groups at different houses. Edson walks across the street to inspect his storehouse, but otherwise sits watching and waiting for something to happen—it rarely does. About once a week a cow is butchered, a task usually performed by Luciano. The women take large basins and buy what fresh meat they want at NCr$ 1 a kilo; the rest of the meat is salted and kept by the animal's owner. Washing clothes is part of the daily routine and the women do this in the river, leaving the clothes spread out over the rocks to dry. A little before ten o'clock Eduardo goes to start the electricity generator so that the *telegrafista* can carry out his morning's communication with Bôa Vista. He then rides around the village on his bicycle to see that the lights in the houses are turned off.

An occasional visitor rides into town, ties up his horse in the shade of one of the small mango trees, and goes first, almost without fail, to pay his respects to Edson, who will invite him to sit down and calls for cold water and coffee to be brought. Jean, probably nursing a hangover, pores over a ledger, trying to remember who bought what on credit the day before. Occasionally someone comes into the shop to buy something, but more often than not just to natter. On most days a light airplane passes overhead on its way to the diamond mines on the Venezuelan frontier, and several times a week one lands at Murusu. It may be the mission's airplane, carrying one of the nuns back from Bôa Vista or bringing in supplies. This airplane always buzzes the mission first and the father drives down in a rather battered jeep to pick up the visitor or stores. More often it is one of the commercial charter planes returning one of the ranchers to the district or bringing in new stock for one of the shopkeepers. Every two weeks, on the days before the FAB flight is due, there are always an extra number of people in town waiting for a free trip into Bôa Vista. Although few people turn out to meet the single-engine airplanes, almost the whole village goes down to the airstrip when the FAB DC-3 arrives.

Lunch is taken between 11 o'clock and noon and by the latter time most people have gone to their hammocks for a siesta. The town looks totally deserted, except for a visitor's horse, with its head hung down, standing in the shade of a tree. A little before 2:30 Eduardo reappears and starts the generator for the second radio transmission of the day. People slowly emerge from their houses, and the groups of people take to forming and reforming again, although now mainly on the western side of the village, where the shade is. As people return from their day's work, the groups swell in size, and the conversation becomes less desultory as men visit the shops for shots of *cachaça*. This is usually taken straight and it is conventional to pull a face after swallowing it. The children come back from school and during the late afternoon the women return to the river to bathe and to collect their dry washing. Toward dusk the men go down to bathe, the local rule being that men may bathe naked from 6:00 P.M. onward. As it grows dark, Eduardo starts the generator yet again and it runs until 9:00 P.M. to provide street and house lighting. Supper is eaten soon after dusk; then there is little left to do but talk, play dominoes, listen to the radio or gramophone, and when the lights go off, go to sleep.

Occasionally a dance is held. This may be a purely spontaneous affair or it may have been planned by someone in order to celebrate his birthday. The dance takes place in someone's house by the light of kerosene pressure lamps, unless it is a big enough occasion for the generator to be left on. Music is more often than not provided by a gramophone, although it is possible to hire musicians, usually *caboclos*, and the party may well go on until the early hours of the morning.

Each day is very similar to the one before; even Sundays can only be differentiated from other days by the occurrence of church services, mainly attended by women. The picture of daily life in Murusu as just portrayed may appear to the reader to be unutterably monotonous and tedious, but for the people who live there the comparison is made between town life and life on the isolated ranches on the savanna. If this comparison is made, then Vila Murusu has considerable intensity of social intercourse; the normal Brazilian terms are *movimento* and *zoada*, which literally mean movement and noise, but are used to refer to the hustle and bustle of city life. Murusu appears to have this—there are shops, drinks (very few people drink on their ranches), almost a crowd of people to talk with, travelers coming and going by horse, jeep, or airplane, a source of information and gossip, a slightly different way of life, and electric lights—the Brazilian backwoodsman's symbol for civilization. But the great event of the year, when visitors even come to Murusu from Bôa Vista, is the annual festival of the patron saint, and this is the subject of the next chapter.

12

Festa

The annual *festa* at Vila Murusu has had a great reputation in the area for many years, even, in fact, before the place was a nucleated settlement. In those days the festival must have been similar in form to that still observable in regions without settlements, where the *festa* takes place at a different ranch each night.

Dispute Concerning Date

The *festa* at Murusu had, until 1967, always been held in March to coincide with the feast of São José, the patron saint of the mission. In 1954 the ranchers and inhabitants of the Murusu region got together and built the present church in the township, which is dedicated to Nossa Senhora do Perpetuo Socorro, who is now the patroness of the town. In 1967 a young Italian father took over at the mission and declared that, since São José is the mission's, and not the town's, patron, his festival would be celebrated simply at the mission, and that if the town wanted a festival, they must have one in commemoration of its patroness, whose day is in December. This caused considerable irritation and animosity among the locals, who declared that moving the date would ruin the *festa*; they argued that in December everybody is busy with roundup and unable to spare the time for a *festa* while in March, at the very end of the dry season, all range work is finished. Another argument was that there are no horses available in December for the races (a key part of the *festa*), since they are all working. Finally, it was argued that a December date clashes with the celebrations for the patroness of Bôa Vista, Nossa Senhora do Carmo, which would prevent any visitors coming from that city, and that it was too close to the annual festival of the Amajari area in January and people certainly would not go to both.

Not all of these arguments are very sound. For example, there are no indications that roundup, which is in full swing in January, stops people from going to the Amajari *festa*. Nor are the horses that are raced the same as those that are used for range work. However, the townsfolk were not entirely unanimous in their condemnation of the father; one man remarked that the Murusu festival had been going downhill for years and was now not nearly so well attended as in the past. Another said that the Amajari festival was anyway much better than the Murusu one, which had been for too long under the domination of the priests, which I take to mean that the religious aspect of the festival has become more pronounced and the secular fun and games much reduced.

The inhabitants of Murusu finally appealed to the *prelazia* in Bôa Vista against the decision of the local priest, but they were not supported. The young priest at the mission finally issued an ultimatum saying that he would hold the masses for Nossa Senhora do Perpetuo Socorro in the town's church in December and the people could do what they liked about the secular part of the festival, and further that in March he would hold the masses for São José at the mission. This statement had the desired effect and at the beginning of November plans went ahead for holding the *festa* in December in conjunction with the religious services for Nossa Senhora do Perpetuo Socorro, a victory for the priest, which clearly emphasizes that the religious aspect is a fundamental part of the festival.

Description

The *festa* is composed of three fairly distinct parts. There is the religious part, the novena in honor of the patron saint, which, together with the actual saint's day, provides a ten-day framework for the festival. It is also the excuse for holding the secular part, the drinking and dancing. The third part, and the one not so far mentioned, is concerned with fund raising and is necessary for the upkeep of the town's church. This last part is the only aspect of the festival that requires any organization, since some arrangements have to be made to ensure that a group of people presents prizes for each evening. The organization of this part is in the hands of Eduardo and its nature will emerge quite clearly from the description of the festival without it being necessary to give any preliminary explanation.

The festival begins nine days before the actual day of the saint to be honored, which is typical of such festivals in Roman Catholicism. The day of Nossa Senhora do Perpetuo Socorro is December 8, so that the first day of the novena is November 29. In 1967 this day, a Wednesday, was stormy, and the only event was a mass in the evening, which was attended by the children from the mission orphanage and one or two of the unmarried girls from the town. Indeed the fact that *festa* had started was not discernible and no extra people had arrived in town. Because of the wet weather, the fund-raising activities of the *festa* scheduled for that evening were postponed, and no other activities took place.

On the following day, after mass at 7:30 P.M., a large apparatus resembling an oversized roulette wheel was set up in front of the church. This roulette wheel consisted of a circle divided into sixty numbered segments and a pointer that could be swung by hand. First the prizes from the previous evening were dealt with. These had all been given by the married women of the *vila*: first prize consisted of a cake, second prize a soap tray and box, and third prize six oranges. Sixty tickets were sold at NCr$ .2 each. Eduardo, who was operating the wheel, swung the pointer and the holder of the ticket with the number it stopped against was the winner of the third prize. After the second and first prizes had been disposed of, the prizes for that evening, which had been given by the nuns and schoolteachers from the mission, were dealt with in the same way. The price of the tickets was raised to NCr$ .5, reflecting the higher quality of the first prize—a cold cooked chicken accompanied by *farofa*. Second prize was a dish of pasties and third prize a tin of *goiabada*. First prize was won by one of the lay assistants from the mission, who returned it to be played for again; tickets this time cost NCr$ .2. The number of people present was small and the same few individuals had to buy nearly all the tickets. That was the limit of the festivities for the second day.

On Friday night, the third day of the novena, very much the same pattern repeated itself. This time the shopkeepers of Murusu provided the prizes and there were enough for it to be judged worth having two runs of three prizes each. Prizes ranged from a live chicken to tins of talcum powder. For the first game tickets were priced at NCr$ .5 each, but there was difficulty in finding buyers for all sixty of them; for the second game the price was dropped to NCr$ .2. That evening the number of people was even lower, since no visitors had yet arrived and some of the normal inhabitants had gone to help with roundup on a neighboring ranch. By this time some people were muttering that the *festa* would be a flop, and even the priest was saying that the locals were not yet accustomed to the *festa* in December, but that things would be better next year. However, some of the more optimistic individuals said that things were always slow to begin with and that it would pick up on Monday.

In fact things did improve on the next day, for around lunchtime a number of people drifted into town and sat around all afternoon drinking beer. The sponsor (*patrocinador*) for the forth evening was the Edson family, but despite their wealth the prizes were not lavish—a petticoat, some bras, a few tobacco pouches, and a tin of talcum powder—mainly, one man suggested, slow-moving stock from Vicente's store. However, there were enough items, together with a few objects left over from the previous evening, for there to be three games. In the first two, tickets were priced at NCr$ .25 and in the third at NCr$ .2. The crowd was big enough and enough beer had been drunk for there to be no difficulty selling the tickets. Even so, when the lottery finished at around 9 o'clock, the festivities did not continue in any form.

On Sunday there was a considerable amount of drinking during the day and the number of people in the township had increased visibly. The atmosphere was further improved by a much better ranges of prizes for the evening's roulette. The sponsors on this evening were the ranchers from the north of the town, and there were enough prizes for there to be three runs of three prizes each. The first prizes were a small goat, a cooked chicken, and a cooked turkey. The price of the tickets for the game with the turkey as first prize, and with a cake and tins of beer as second and third prizes respectively, was NCr$ 1. The young goat was won by a *caboclo*, who was immediately offered (with little option to refuse) NCr$ 5 for it by the *guarda*.

After the lottery there was a dance in Eduardo's shop, but there was a shortage of women and the scramble to get a partner at the beginning of each dance was even worse than usual. The etiquette at dances is for the women to sit or stand around the edge of the dance floor and the men to congregate in a huddle at one end of the room, usually near the door. When the music starts, a man approaches the woman with whom he wishes to dance and holds out his hand to her. At the end of the dance they separate and return to their respective places, often without a word passing between them. The shortage of women on this evening meant that men were pointing at their hoped-for partners from the far side of the room at the first beat of music and struggling to get to them first.

Monday passed much as Sunday had, although by now there were enough people in town for there to be several conversation groups. The main topic of conversation was the forthcoming needle race between the "thoroughbred" horses of two local ranchers. The evening saw the usual lottery game after mass. This time the prizes were given by the ranchers from the area to the east, and the main ones were a cooked chicken and a young goat. After the game was over, there was a dance in one of the unoccupied houses; the music was provided by a band of *caboclo* musicians playing an accordion, two guitars, and a tambourine. The dance was given by the *guarda*, which meant that he paid the musicians. Two new features marked the evening: the selling of lemonade and popcorn by a *caboclo* and his wife during the lottery game and the sale of coffee by the family of Luciano, Edson's brother-in-law, during the dancing.

The days by now had taken on an almost routine appearance, with people sitting around talking and drinking in the morning, spending several hours in the middle of the day in their hammocks, and dancing until 3:00 A.M. in the morning. An occasional horse race accompanied by a little gambling or perhaps an attempt to ride a wild mule broke into this routine. On Tuesday one of the visitors, the worse for drink, attempted to rape a married woman after his efforts to seduce her with presents had failed. The *guarda* locked him up in the jail and invited people to come and look at him. Once he was sober he was let out and told to go home. That evening the policeman made his second arrest of the day when a drunken *caboclo* interrupted the dancing. The sponsors for the day's lottery were the ranchers from the area to the south of the town, and the prizes included, as well as the usual cold chicken and turkey, a colt and a sheep.

The dance followed the same pattern as the one the night before. The same empty house was used, the dancers and the band were indoors, and the spectators stood or sat around outside. Some chairs were brought out and many of the older men sat in these talking and listening to the music, while their wives stood behind them. With one exception, there was no close chaperoning of the girls by their mothers, although the girls themselves chaperone each other, never leaving the vicinity of the dance without a companion. Married women have complete freedom to join in the dancing as much as they wish, and although men always drink at dances, that evening was the first occasion that I had ever seen Murusu women drinking. One of the ranchers bought a bottle of beer for his wife and she and another woman retired indoors to drink it. Women are not expected to drink but unbeknownst to their husbands many do, Jean being always ready to supply them secretly.

Wednesday, the eighth day, passed without any disturbance. There were some horse races on the flat piece of land between the town and the mission, but no other form of entertainment until the evening. The providers of the prizes were the ranchers from the area to the northwest of the town; one of the first prizes was a saddle, an item that pushed the price of the tickets up to NCr$ 2. Two dances were held that evening—a "smart" one in Luciano's house, at which the music was provided by gramophone, and one in Zecão's shop, with music from a *caboclo* band. The attendance at these respective dances clearly portrayed the main division of Roraima society into *civilizado* and *caboclo*. None of the white girls went to Zecão's and no *caboclos* of either sex to Luciano's, but many white men went to both and some of them spent the whole time at Zecão's, where they competed on equal footing with the *caboclos* for dancing partners.

Everybody was up early on Thursday, the penultimate day of the *festa*, in order to watch the big race that was run soon after 6:30 A.M. There had been much talk of large bets being laid, but when it came to it only very small sums of money changed hands. Drinking started straight after the race, few people

Horseracing during the festa *at Murusu.*

showed much interest in the other races, and at 8:00 A.M. a dance started in the house of Antônio, which went on until noon. The afternoon was quiet but desultory drinking started as soon as the siesta was over. This evening the lottery prizes were given by the ranchers of the Parime region, to the southwest of the town, and included a colt, two heifers, and a sheep; the last only rated as a second prize. A dance was given by José, Edson's brother-in-law. It was held in Edson's storehouse and carpenter's shop, one of the best buildings in Murusu for this purpose, having wide doors and windows. The band was composed of *caboclos* as usual, but this evening a *civilizado* occasionally joined in. At 1:00 A.M. food— cold chicken and *farofa*—was provided and the dance continued without a break until breakfast time.

This was the saint's day, and following on the night's strenuous activity, it passed quietly. The culmination of the religious part of the *festa* took place in the late afternoon. Mass was said at about 5:00 P.M. and was a little better attended than usual. After the service was over, the image of the saint was brought out and processed round the town. The procession was composed of most of the townspeople, visitors, and the children from the mission orphanage. It was headed by a boy carrying a cross, behind him came the other boys, then the girls, women, and nuns, after them the priest, and finally the saint, carried on a stretcher at shoulder height by four men and with all the other men surrounding them. The procession went from the church down one side of the main street to the air-strip and back up the other, circumambulating in an anticlockwise direction.

The procession of the saint did not take long and as soon as the image was safely back in the church, the roulette wheel was set up for the final evening's play. The sponsors on this last evening were the authorities, which in-cluded the federal governor, the municipal government, and the local government officials. The presents were of a high standard and included calves for the first time.

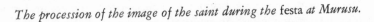

The procession of the image of the saint during the festa *at Murusu.*

Two dances took place that night—a *caboclo* one in Zecão's place, although this time to gramophone music, and one in the carpenter's shop, with the *caboclo* musicians. Both events were well attended (although continuing to show the social distinctions already mentioned), but they lacked the spontaneous high spirits of the previous night's entertainment. By 4:00 A.M. both dances had finished and the *festa* at Murusu was over for another year. Daylight revealed a hung-over town littered with paper and empty beer bottles and tins and already half deserted, since many had mounted their horses and set off back to their ranches as soon as the last step had been danced.

In spite of initial doubts and the fact that the total takings at the lottery (NCr$ 700) were slightly down from the previous year, the *festa* was judged to have been a success.

Discussion

A number of points, some obvious and others less obvious, may be made about this *festa*. While the town at any time of year offers greater animation than the isolated savanna dwellings, during the period of the *festa* this activity is increased. Although an occasional visit to town during the year allows the rancher to meet friends and acquaintances by chance, the *festa* ensures that everyone from the neighborhood will be in town. Thus the *festa* provides an opportunity for reaffirming old ties and is a mechanism for social reintegration and lubrication. This does not mean that this ritual period is always one of social harmony. Although the *festa* I attended was peaceful, the Roraimaenses expect that there will be fighting at dances. The *festa* simply provides the socially sanctioned excuse for getting together; it cannot dictate how people will behave once they are together.

As was mentioned at the beginning of this chapter, the excuse for holding the festival and the framework in which it operates are basically religious. For example, the townsfolk, because they could not visualize holding a purely secular festival, lost their argument with the priest over the date of the *festa*. In spite of this, the main interest is in the secular events and except for the procession of the saint's image, the religious functions are poorly attended. If the whole period of the *festa* may be seen as a ritual period in which there is a heightening of religious and secular activity that are complementary to each other, then the importance of the procession of the saint's image, the culmination of the religious part of the *festa*, may be understood as the greatest intrusion of the sacred into the profane. This point is further stressed by the fact that it is the grown men, a class that normally takes the least part in spiritual affairs, who carry the image on their shoulders.

If the nightly lottery is looked at in the same way, that is to say as an expression of a relationship between the sacred and profane worlds, some interesting features emerge. The whole game is one of chance (like the socioeconomic system), but it is held in order to obtain money for religious purposes, for the upkeep of the church. It is held at dusk (neither night nor day), in front of the church, and with the priest and nuns present. The atmosphere in which it is conducted contrasts plainly both with the sacred character of the religious service that precedes it and with the profane nature of the dances that follow it. For example, the lottery tickets are sold by young unmarried girls, who, in order to do so, mingle freely with the crowd, which is also mixed. I found that on these occasions girls to whom I had barely spoken before exchanged banter with me. The relative freedom between sexes during the lottery contrasts vividly with their separation in the church and their alternating separation and conjunction at the dance.

The temporary abeyance of certain structural distinctions during the lottery suggests that this period has certain liminal qualities; through them may be revealed certain values that are not otherwise expressed. The main characteristic of the lottery is that, unlike any other part of the *festa*, it has an organization. Compared with festivals in some other Latin American countries, this organization is of a very low order and there is apparently no hierarchy of offices nor competition for them. Indeed, the organization does little more than arrange for there to be prizes on each evening of the festival. Furthermore, it is declared explicitly that there is no competition between the various sponsors to see who can provide the most lavish prizes. This is said to be impossible because many people belong to more than one designated group, and this is true. For example, Vicente, Edson's eldest son, is a member of Edson family, a Murusu shopkeeper, and a rancher from the region to the east of the town. This claim to a noncompetitive and egalitarian organization does not fit with certain of the observed facts. As the novena progressed, the prizes became steadily better and this is directly attributable to the fact that the sponsors chosen for the early evenings of the festival, when the crowds are small, are those who are not in a position to provide good prizes. The sponsors for the evenings later in the novena have greater prestige and status and the prizes they give get increasingly better, the best prizes being given on the final evening. There is, then, a hierarchical arrangement within the organization of the lottery, and one can relate to this the fact that many individuals took no notice of the organization and gave prizes on a night sponsored by a group of which they were not a member, or if they belonged to several groups they chose one evening rather than another. A definite pattern emerged in this behavior and those who did not give a prize on the night of their group invariably gave it on a later night (never an earlier one) or if they belonged to several groups would select a later rather than earlier date. It would seem that these people are making statements about their ranking. The best example is Edson, who gave nothing on the various days on which groups of which he is a member were sponsors, but on the saint's day itself, for which the officially designated sponsors were the authorities, he provided a calf, one of only two that were offered as prizes during the whole *festa*. It was this example that made me look closely at the system, because Edson, who is not an authority, has *de facto* control of the area.

There does seem to be here a way of making a claim to a position or rank in a hierarchy that is neither institutionalized nor fully recognized. The failure of the participants either to be aware of (or, perhaps, admit to) this embryonic ranking system may be attributable to the same reason as that which accounts for only partial awareness of the system of patronage associated with *sorte*, that is to say, commitment to an egalitarian ideology blocks recognition of such contradictory phenomena.

13

Change

In earlier chapters attention has been concentrated on the traditional methods and techniques of ranching in Roraima, but throughout it has been indicated that these traits are not practiced uniformly through the region and that modernization and development are coming to the territory. In this final chapter it is intended to discuss both the factors that hold back the ranching industry of Roraima, and the factors that will result in its change.

Obstacles to Development

Many of the problems that face the territory spring from the nature of the environment, in particular the geographical isolation and the climatic regime. The environmental factors influence the form of the socioeconomic organization of the territory directly and also act upon it indirectly through their effect on communications. The problems presented are very real, but one cannot fail to question whether they are as overwhelming as the ranchers themselves claim. The practical problems facing the area are known by virtually every Roraimaense and are a constant topic of conversation. It would be interesting to know how far the Roraimaenses have worked out these difficulties for themselves and how far they have been adopted from the various publications on the territory, all of which repeat the same points. Whichever it is, these problems have now been built into what I shall refer to as a self-justifying model of backwardness. The model operates in this way: the various difficulties facing the development of the region are used to account for the backwardness of the area, and then backwardness is given, tautologically, to account for the problems. When one asks why the region is underdeveloped, the answer is the problems which it faces; when one asks why these problems cannot be overcome, one is referred to the backwardness of the area.

Alongside this self-justifying model of backwardness exist the remedies for the situation. These remedies almost invariably stipulate external help and do not recommend a cure by the application of self-help and greater effort within the community. Indeed, given the self-justifying model of backwardness, the egalitarian values, and the social disapproval directed at anyone who is ambitious or goes beyond the traditional system, it is hardly surprising that the Roraimaense looks outside his system for help. However, this is not to deny that there is some basic truth in his views, since we have already seen the severe practical and economic difficulties which face the rancher who might wish to develop his business. The proposed remedy is government support, in fact the injection of large sums of money to improve communications and subsidize such things as barbed wire, mineral salts, the building of dams to provide irrigated pastures, and bulls for breeding. It is clear that all these things would result in an improvement in the ranching industry's productivity and equally certain that at least some government assistance will be needed if these things are to be introduced. However, real development, rather than the traditional system being maintained by large loans, will require a change in some deeply entrenched values and attitudes.

One of the themes running through this study has been the existence of conscious egalitarian values and practices that give rise to an unconscious hierarchical order. This is very well revealed in the system of *sorte*, which involves the fostering of another's socioeconomic rise to the detriment of one's own economic advancement. While this system allows the expression of egalitarian ideals, at the same time it disguises a hierarchical structure which is implicit in any form of patronage. Upward mobility is a built-in part of the system and with a degree of hard work and a modicum of luck any *vaqueiro* will end up a *fazendeiro*, the equal of his employer. The man may economically outstrip his patron, but as has been noted the relationship of patron and client is expressed in physiological terms. This has two effects: firstly, it means that a client cannot become superior to his patron, just as a son cannot change places with his father; and secondly, by expressing the relationship in a "natural" mode, one disguises its basically hierarchical character. The system is beautifully balanced, since it allows for the expression of egalitarian ideals, while hiding a hierarchical ordering of socioeconomic relationships. Together they form the ladder to the status to which the community has granted the greatest prestige, and the means for climbing it. This unconscious model of society provides an interesting contrast with the conscious model of backwardness, for while the latter is tautologous, the former is contradictory; and it is unconscious because the various elements of it are never juxtaposed by the Roraimaenses. The conscious model is founded on a number of concretely observable factors and the unconscious model on a set of attitudes that contains the organizational principles of the ranching society.

It is claimed that the obstacles to development are to be found more in the attitudes and ideology contained in the unconscious model than in the practical difficulties that face economic development and that are the basis of the self-justifying model of backwardness. However, one must be very careful not to push these models too far apart, since they are both rooted in the same facts. The superstructure of ideas has its roots in the peculiar and particular aspects of the environmental infrastructure. Indeed, in this area, the relationship between the nature of the environment, the socioeconomic organization, and the system of ideas is exceptionally clear. This is not to say that the traditional values will prevent change but they will certainly slow it down. Progress means an efficient, money-oriented ranching industry and this is incompatible with the treasured ideals of many of the ranching people of Roraima. Change is taking place in the area at an ever-increasing rate and we will now go on to consider some of the factors and agencies involved in this change.

Factors Producing Change

For analytical purposes two sets of factors and agencies can be recognized, although, as will be seen, they are not exclusive sets. They are the internal factors and the external ones.

The single most important internal factor working toward change in Roraima is related to land. The socioeconomic system that has grown up in Roraima depends for its continuation on an unlimited supply of land. The *vaqueiro* who has made good needs land on which to set up his own ranch— this land is traditionally free. Although, because no cadastral survey of the territory has been made nor any systematic record of land ownership kept, it is not known how much empty land there is left, nearly everyone spoken to was of the opinion that there is very little. In spite of this, and perhaps this exemplifies the attitude to land, its supply is not something that arouses any concern. Although I heard most of the economic problems facing the territory spontaneously (and frequently) discussed, the only occasions on which land and its supply were talked about were when I introduced the topic, and it never excited much interest then. The fact that the system of payment by *sorte*, and thus ultimately the socioeconomic life, relies on a constant supply of free land did not seem to occur to them; land is quite simply not within the class of limited goods. However, once there is no empty land left, some change will have to take place.

There are a number of possible results. Ranching will become less and less of an economic business, since *vaqueiros* may just continue to run their growing herds with the rancher's. This will destroy the potential upward mobility, since it will prevent the *vaqueiro* from becoming a *fazendeiro* in his own right because this status depends on owning a ranch. It might be possible for the *vaqueiro* to buy a ranch, but this requires more money than is available to a young rising *vaqueiro*. Those who buy ranches are those who are already successful ranchers or those who have made money elsewhere—in commerce, diamond mining, or politics. Furthermore, with the disappearance of empty lands, the Brazilian inheritance laws will bite harder and the size of landholdings will begin to diminish. This will have an adverse effect on the ranching industry, for which large units are economically best.

The answer to these difficulties will almost certainly be that the rancher will start paying wages to his *vaqueiro*. Some of the larger ranching concerns in the territory already pay their men in wages, but this system of payment will have far-reaching socioeconomic effects if and when widely adopted. It has already been mentioned that the *vaqueiro* dislikes wage payment because it makes it very difficult (perhaps impossible, since no example was found) to achieve the status of rancher, an expectation and goal that exist in the minds of all Roraima cattlemen. Wage payment will turn the embryonic ranchers into a rural proletariat and there will develop a gulf between *fazendeiro* and *vaqueiro*, which at the moment does not exist. The disappearance of the frontier, in the sense of an unlimited supply of empty land, will almost certainly give rise to a wage economy, which, in turn, will result in the destruction of the egalitarian attitudes that are such a universal feature of the frontier situation. However, this is a slightly hypothetical discussion, since it seems unlikely that the effect of land shortage alone will have the chance to work itself out. External factors are operating that are likely to bring about a similar result sooner.

The major external factor comes under the heading of improved communications. The most important improvement is that between the territory and its markets. The discussion of a land link between Bôa Vista and Manaus has been going on for eighty years, and the present plan is to build a road that will form part of the major network that will join Rio de Janeiro and Caracas. Given the present record of road building in Brazil and the fact that work on the road has already started, it seems likely that the territory's long wait for a road connection with the rest of the country is almost over. The effects of this road will be enormous and numerous; many of them perhaps unforeseeable. But as far as the economy of the territory is concerned, the road will have some obvious repercussions. Firstly, there is the far greater ease with which goods will be transported into the region, which should have an effect on price, variety, and year-round availability. Secondly, the transport of cattle to market will greatly improve—not only will it be possible to transship cattle all the year round, but the system of shipment should ensure that the cattle, and thus the meat, will arrive at market in far better condition. This, in turn, should make it worthwhile to produce a better quality of beef.

Once it is possible to send cattle to market at any time of year, the question that is likely to arise is whether or not there are enough cattle available to meet the demand. Under the traditional (and to a great extent present) system a rancher loses 25 percent of his production in wages. In fact, the situation is worse than this since these "lost" animals are pastured in competition with the rancher's own herd. A greater demand for cattle for market will certainly give impetus toward paying cowhands in cash, which, although to the detriment of the *vaqueiro*, will under the new conditions become advantageous to the rancher. The reverse side of this, and a factor that will further encourage the growth of a wage economy, is that improved transport will vastly increase the number and range of consumer goods available in the territory.

Consumer goods outside a very narrow range are missing from the traditional economy of the ranching community. However, the problem is not simply a lack of goods but also the lack of a market, and this was apparent in the description of Murusu. Although the township arose in response to a need for education, its existence created an agglomeration of people large enough to support a number of shops. These shops are interesting because they have a foot in both camps; they are tied to the money-oriented economy of the external world but operate in the middle of an economy that is not money oriented. In fact, one of the problems on the savannas is that money is physically in short supply —it is frequently impossible to get change for a NCr$ 5 note. In the setting of Murusu it is interesting to note that the traditional cattle economy still has the upper hand and that the shopkeeper who has the largest turnover and profit is the one who goes furthest to accept the traditional system and will take cattle in lieu of cash.

Improved communications are not going to mean just easier marketing of cattle and more consumer goods; they will also lead to changes in outlook. Ten years of jeeps and transistor radios have done much in this way, and a wider perspective on life is reinforced by the availability of such Brazilian periodicals as *Cruzeiro* and *Manchete*, which contain advertisements and photographs of a glamorous world beyond the savanna edge. If good Americans used to go to Paris when they died, the Brazilian of the interior dreams of Rio de Janeiro and Copacabana beach.

The easiest steps for the rancher to take in order to turn from the traditional to the market economy are to stop paying wages in cattle and to restrict the grazing on his land to his own herd. The next steps are more problematic and will require some sort of financial subsidy, since not even the largest ranching concerns of the territory have the capital to carry out the development that is required. Most of the necessary actions have already been discussed, but basically they come down to improving the breed so that the cattle weigh more and take a shorter time in reaching a marketable weight and so that the resulting meat is of a better quality. In fact, many of the traditional ranchers would like to see such a development in the ranching industry, without discarding the traditional system of payment. Experience from other rather similar situations (in northeast and central Brazil) indicate, however, that this rarely happens and as each head of cattle becomes more valuable, not simply in itself but as a result of its improved marketability, the system of *sorte* gradually changes from one in four to one in five or one in six, so that the *vaqueiro*'s pay, although still in cattle, is adjusted like a cash wage.

In order to improve the breed it will also be necessary to improve the pasturage of the savannas—this means sown grasses, which in turn depend on fencing and, in many parts, irrigation. Better quality meat must have a better means of transport than that used at the moment, and one is back with the need for improved communications. However, if the territory as a whole is going to benefit from improvements in the ranching industry, it will be necessary to do something about the extractive nature of the industry. By this we are not referring to the attitude of the rancher toward his cattle, but rather to the fact that at the moment all cattle for market leave Roraima on the hoof. In other words, Roraima loses all the advantages from processing by-products of the meat industry. There would seem to be enormous scope for the development of a by-products industry—beef canning and extracts, a leather industry, and so forth— and given the difficulties of exporting cattle, it seems astonishing that no such industry has grown up in Bôa Vista in conjunction with the shipment of meat by air. The use of air transport in this way has been tried successfully in many remote parts of the world, including neighboring Guyana. The Rupununi savannas of Guyana suffer a similar problem in communication, but since 1955 Guyana Airways, using DC-3s, have been airlifting out the carcasses of cattle slaughtered in the interior. The use of air transport has only been attempted once in Roraima, as a private venture by the largest ranching concern. It did not last long because the aircraft available, a Catalina that carried too little and a Lodestar that carried too much, proved uneconomical. The failure of the project would seem to be the result of an unwillingness to cooperate with other ranchers. Symptomatic of the same malaise are the facts that a new abattoir built in 1948 is still not operating and that shortage of meat is a recurrent problem in Bôa Vista. The problem here is one of internal politics. Although we have refrained from examining this subject, in discussing change and development in the territory, it is essential to indicate this as an important element.

It would be wrong to be too certain about the development prospects of Roraima—past schemes have failed hopelessly. A present development aid that would not seem to have any future is the inclusion of Bôa Vista in mid-1969 in the Manaus Free Trade Zone. It would seem merely to be making legal the present illegal import of goods into the city, and may well have the effect of reducing the profits on a very thriving smuggling industry. However, with the real possibility of a road connecting the territory with Manaus, and the rest of Brazil in due course, the development of the territory seems just around the corner, and with it will come a money economy. Wages seem an inevitable concomitant of a market economy and both are antipathetical to an egalitarian ideology. The traditional methods of ranching are already doomed, and after them, the related set of values and attitudes. When these have gone, Roraima and her cattlemen will have succumbed to the fate of all frontiers.

Glossary

AFFINES: Relatives by marriage.

Afilhado, –a: Godson, goddaughter.

Barracão: Bunkhouse.

Branco: Literally, white; used to refer to all those who are of non-Amerindian parentage and culture.

Caatinga: Scrubland bush of northeastern Brazil.

Caboclo: Nontribal Amerindian.

Cafezinho: Small cup of sweet black coffee.

Capataz: The manager of a ranch or outstation.

Cachaça: Rum.

Civilizado: Those who are not of Amerindian background and culture.

Comadre: Term used by parents to their child's godmother, and by her to the child's mother.

Comboiero: Drover, or man who accompanies an ox-train.

Compadre: Term used by parents to their child's godfather, and by him to the child's father.

Compadresco: Relationships between parents and godparents and between godparents and godchildren. Ritual kinship.

CONSANGUINEOUS RELATIONS: Those related to each other by descent or blood, rather than by marriage (*affines*).

Delegado: Sheriff.

Farinha: Manioc flour.

Farofa: *Farinha* fried with oil or fat and mixed with pieces of meat, onion, and so forth.

Fazenda: Ranch.

Fazendeiro: Rancher.

Garimpo: Diamond mine or minings.

Garimpeiro: Diamond miner.

Goiabada: Guava cheese.

Gripe: Any form of nose, throat, or chest ailment.

Guarda: Guard, policeman.

Lavrado: Flat, treeless plain.

Lote: Herd of cattle, the animals of which live on the same pasture.

Madrinha: Godmother.

Maloca: Indian village or settlement.

Morador: Settler or smallholder.

Motorista: Engineer, mechanic.

NEOLOCAL RESIDENCE: The practice of married couples taking up residence away from both sets of parents.

NUCLEAR FAMILY: A family consisting of parents and their unmarried children.

Padrinho: Godfather.

Palmo: The distance covered between the thumb and small finger of the outstretched hand (about twenty-two centimeters).

Retiro: Outstation of a ranch.

Sede: Main center of a ranch.

Sitio: Smallholding.

Vaqueiro: The man on a ranch who is in charge of the cattle.

References

BELSHAW, C. S., 1965, *Traditional Exchange and Modern Markets.* Englewood Cliffs, N. J.: Prentice-Hall.

COUDREAU, H., 1887, *La France équinoxiale*, Vol. 2, "Voyage à travers les Guyanes et l'Amazonie." Paris: Challamel aîné.

DINIZ, E. S., 1966, "O Perfil de uma Situação Interétnica," *Boletim do Museu Paraense Emilio Goeldi*, Antropologia No. 31.

FIRTH, R., 1956, *Elements of Social Organization.* London: Watts.

FOSTER, G. M., 1965, "Peasant Society and the Image of Limited Good," *American Anthropologist*, 67:293–315.

PEREIRA, L., 1917, *O Rio Branco.* Manaus, Brazil: Imprensa Publica.

DE SOUZA, A. F., 1848, "Notícias geographicas da capitania do Rio Negro no grande Rio Amazonas," *Revista trimensal de Historia e Geographia*, 3 (2nd Series): 411–504.

STRICKON, A., 1965, "The Euro-American Ranching Complex," in A. Leeds and A. P. Vayda, eds., *Man, Culture, and Animals.* Washington, D.C.: American Association for the Advancement of Science, Publication 78. Pp. 229–258.

WAGLEY, C., AND M. HARRIS, 1955, "A Typology of Latin American Subcultures," *American Anthropologist*, 57:428–451.

WOLF, E. R., 1955, "Types of Latin American Peasantry: A Preliminary Discussion," *American Anthropologist*, 57:452–471.

Additional Readings

The Brazilian Case in the Boundary Dispute with Great Britain, 1903. First Memoir, Annexes 1–5, and Second Memoir, Vols. 1–3, Annexes 1–3. London: Foreign Office.

The British Case in the Boundary Dispute with Brazil, 1903. Annexes 1–4. London: Foreign Office.

The Notes to the British Counter-Case in the Boundary Dispute with Brazil, 1903. London: Foreign Office. This and the volumes above reproduce most of the important documents and accounts of Roraima prior to 1900.

DINIZ, E. S., 1966, "O perfil de uma situação interétnica," *Boletim do Museu Paraense Emilio Goeldi,* Antropologia No. 31. Deals with the relationship between *civilizados* and *caboclos.*

EVANS-PRITCHARD, E. E., 1940, *The Nuer.* Oxford: Clarendon Press. The classic account of African pastoralists.

GUERRA, A. T., 1957, *Estudo Geográfico do Território do Rio Branco.* Rio de Janeiro: Instituto Brasileiro de Geografia e Estatística, Conselho Nacional de Geografia. A good geographical account of Roraima, with detailed descriptions of soil, climate, geomorphology, and so forth.

McGill University Savanna Research Project. This project relates to the Rupununi savanna of Guyana, the region adjacent to Roraima. The findings already published cover a wide range of topics.

MASCARENHAS, H. AND ROZENTAL, M., 1966, *Aspectos da Indústria Pastoril do Território do Rio Branco.* Rio de Janeiro: Ministério da Agricultura. Contains recommendations for the development of the cattle industry in Roraima.

MOREIRA NETO, C. A., 1960, "A cultural pastoril do Páu d'Arco," *Boletim do Museu Paraense Emilio Goeldi,* Antropologia No. 10. Deals with the growth and condition of the cattle industry in a frontier region of central Brazil (Rio Araguaia).

NAIPAUL, V. S., 1962, *The Middle Passage.* London: Andre Deutsch. Contains a brilliant description of Bôa Vista, pp. 104–112.

OSGOOD, E. S., 1929, *The Day of the Cattleman.* Minneapolis: University of Minnesota Press. An excellent general account of the North American cattle frontier, 1870–1900.

SMITH, H. H., 1966, *The War on Powder River.* New York: McGraw-Hill. A detailed and sober account of an incident on the American cattle frontier.